MASS COMMUNICATIONS

TEXAS TECH STYLE

Bill Dean

Texas Tech University

Kendall Hunt
publishing company
4050 Westmark Drive • P O Box 1840 • Dubuque IA 52004-1840

Cover image courtesy of Texas Tech Office of Communications and Marketing.

Kendall Hunt
publishing company
www.kendallhunt.com
Send all inquiries to:
4050 Westmark Drive
Dubuque, IA 52004-1840

Printed in the United States of America
10 9 8 7 6 5 4 3 2

Contents

Overview   v

UNIT I

1 The Communications Process As It Relates to the News Media   **3**

2 Political, Economic, and Social Importance of Mass Media   **7**

3 Freedom of the Press   **11**

UNIT II

4 Growth of the Press   **29**

5 Newspapers   **37**

6 Magazines   **49**

UNIT III

7 Growth of Broadcasting   **61**

8 Radio   **73**

9 Television   **79**

UNIT IV

10 The Media's Social and Ethical Responsibilities   **97**

11 Credibility   **101**

12 Advertising   **111**

13 Public Relations   **119**

Overview

Overview of Course

Thesis

American mass media—newspapers, magazines, radio and television—come as close to being universal in scope and coverage as any other institutional force in the country.

Newspapers

Newspapers have been a part of American history since 1690. The first regularly published paper was in 1704, and they have kept a record of our history ever since. In recent times newspapers have brought us historic news like the resignation of President Nixon that was brought about by the Watergate scandal or the 9-11 attacks.

1. For many years the number of daily newspapers changed little. With the coming of the Internet, newspapers have experienced a drop in readers and a drop in advertising. There are approximately 1,452 dailies with a circulation exceeding 52 million. Both figures are down from five years ago. There are approximately 7,000 weekly papers with a circulation of 63.5 million.

2. The average size newspaper is about 20,000 circulation.

3. A total of 124 million read the newspaper every day.

4. The average reader spends 45 minutes a day.

Magazines

Magazines play a role in America's social, political, and cultural life. Henry Luce started the first news magazine, *Time,* in 1923. Killed off in advertising wars were *Collier's, Saturday Evening Post, Life* and *Look,* popular mass circulation magazines. Today we have thousands of specialized magazines.

1. There are some 31,000-plus periodicals published in the U.S. exceeding 358 billion circulation.

2. Of these only 600 are classified as general interest.

3. Included in the total figure are some 13,000 house organs, trade publications, industrial, and company publications.

4. An average of 89% of American adults read at least one magazine regularly.

Books

1. Some 2,000 publishing firms produce more than 50,000 new titles each year.

2. Books are read by about one in five of the adults in this country on a regular basis.

Radio

In the 1930s, 1940s, and 1950s the family gathered around the radio for comedy shows, big name bands, their favorite news commentator, or a sporting event.

1. Of the 13,977 radio stations, 4,776 are AM, while 6,309 are FM. There are another 2,892 educational FM stations. FM has 71% of the audience. FM has 81% of the audience aged 12–24. An average of 88% of all adults listen every day.

2. It is estimated that nearly 100% of all American homes have a radio (average 6.6).

3. The average family listens approximately 2 hours and 15 minutes a day.

Television

With the coming of TV, families now gathered around the TV to watch Milton Berle or Ed Sullivan. Television has had considerable impact on other media. Its programming has been controversial at times. In the 1970s we had the so-called "family hours" and "an effort to clean up prime time." The issue of whether exposure to so much crime and violence has a negative impact on children has been debated for a long time. Every evening at least 50 million Americans watch network news and 75 million (many of course the same) watch local TV news. Cameras and microphones blitz us with images and sounds.

1. There are 1,747 TV stations: 700 VHF, 1,000 UHF, and 364 Public.

2. There are 7,832 cable systems in the country and there are 65.2 million cable homes and 28 million DBS satellite homes out of a potential 110 million homes (85%). At least 20 million also take a pay service.

3. An average of 99% of all homes have a TV set and 98% are color.

4. The average family watches 8 hours and 21 minutes a day. Network viewing in prime time has dropped to a share of only 50% from 93% in 1978.

5. Studies indicate that a TV household watches nearly 50 hours each week, but households with children tune in for about 60 hours a week.

6. In general, women view more than men; older men and women view more than younger age groups, and young children view more than older children and teens.

7. Sunday is the night TV is watched most; Monday was runner-up; 8:30–9 P.M.

8. February is the highest month; July the lowest.

9. More than 120 million people viewed at least part of last year's Super Bowl game. On that program commercials cost over one million dollars per 30 seconds.

Films

Social critics argue about the effects of movies. But some classics speak for themselves, like *Gone With the Wind*. In the 1970s we had *All the President's Men*, the study of Watergate. All of a sudden every student wanted to become an investigative reporter.

1. Approximately 30% of American adults attend a movie once a month.
2. Of that total 25% are under 20 while 80% are under 40.

Advertising and Public Relations

We will study both the effects and impact that advertising and public relations have on the media and on our society. Advertising has been the object of great concern as far back as the first published ads. As advertising agencies grew into multimillion-dollar operations, they developed some classic ads. Today, we have ads for everything. Ads poke into every part of our lives.

Public Relations

Public relations is another area we will study. While advertising tries to sell products, goods and services, public relations attempts to sell ideas, attitudes and images. Propaganda, a tool of every government, is an effort to influence.

Technology

Obviously, changing technology has greatly impacted the media.

1. Videotape was revolutionary because it can be erased and reused, an important economic factor.
2. Newsgathering is greatly enhanced because videotape is much easier to edit than older 16mm film that was used in the early days of TV.
3. It is common to tape TV programs.
4. Selling videotapes of motion pictures has become a major source of income for the film industry.
5. Computers not only have expanded and speeded up the processes of publication and broadcast, but also have created new, more informal types of communication. A reporter inputs a story into his Video Display Terminal. The story can be edited on the screen and can be recalled by others for checking. This eliminates the need for a typesetter. Computers have given us e-mail and electronic bulletin boards.
6. Using telephone lines, it is now possible to transmit memos, charts, public relations news releases, etc. Some problems exist when unwanted messages, such as a sales pitch, are transmitted.
7. The use of satellites and relay stations has truly revolutionized the transmission of messages and pictures around the world. Transmission by satellite is cheaper, faster and more reliable than by ground lines. Satellites have given us faster news transmission and have promoted the growth of cable TV.

The Internet

1. Today the Internet links millions of academic, governmental and commercial sites.

2. No one owns the Internet.

3. It is a loose collection of computer networks whose users pass along information and share files.

4. Costs are shared rather informally by a variety of institutions.

Convergence

Convergence brings together print and electronic media. Journalism schools today are attempting to train a student to be able to write a news story for the newspaper, then prepare the story to be delivered on air and, finally, to post it up on a Web page.

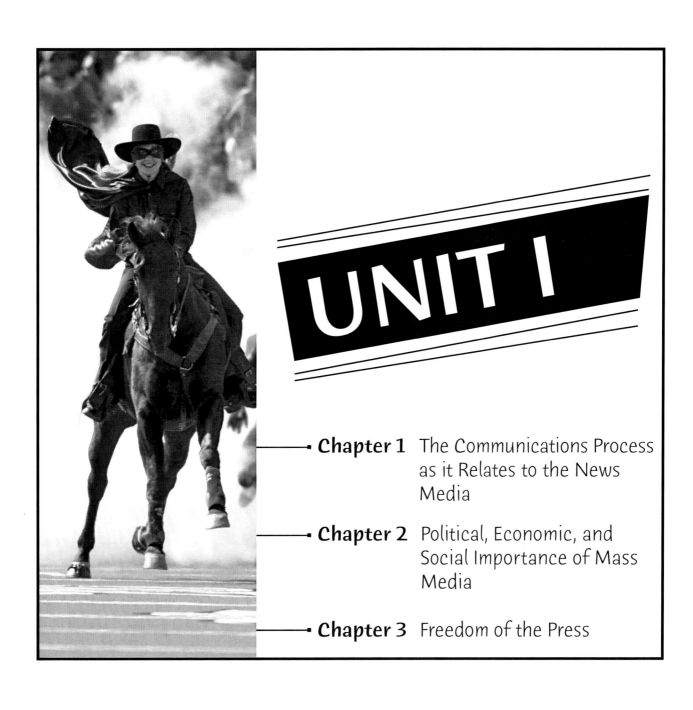

UNIT I

Chapter 1 The Communications Process as it Relates to the News Media

Chapter 2 Political, Economic, and Social Importance of Mass Media

Chapter 3 Freedom of the Press

1 The Communications Process As It Relates to the News Media

Introduction

Definition of Communication Terms

1. The art of transmitting information, ideas, and attitudes from one person to another.

2. Each person communicates with another by directing a message to one or more of the senses.
   a. Sight
   b. Sound
   c. Touch
   d. Taste
   e. Smell

3. Interpersonal communication is communicating to others while intrapersonal communication represents our private thoughts and ideas.

4. But our society is too complex to rely on direct communication between one individual and another. Thus we turn to mass communications.

5. Mass communications is the art of transmitting information, ideas, and attitudes to reach a sizable and diversified audience through the use of the media.

The Communication Process

1. The communicator
2. The message
3. The channel
4. The audience

Communicator ←————————→ Audience
Channel
Message

Problems

1. **Channel Noise**—distractions between C and A—overcome by use of attention-getting devices and through redundancy.

2. **Semantic Noise**—misunderstood even though received—overcome by trying to select terms and words within the audience's frame of reference. Also—a word may mean one thing to C and another to A. The dictionary meaning is called DENOTATIVE. The emotional or evaluative meaning is called CONNOTATIVE.

    Take pains to define terms and adjust vocabulary to the interests and needs of the audience. FACT—the average daily newspaper is geared to an 8th grade vocabulary level.

3. **Stored Experience**—everyone has stored experience. It represents the experiences we have had over our lifetimes that cause us to have certain beliefs and values. Someone might simply reject a message completely because it goes against his or her belief system. Careful research of the audience is important to try and overcome this problem.

4. **Dissonance**—inconsistent actions that are contrary to the way a person or a group normally behaves. Every now and then we do something or say something that is totally inconsistent with what we normally do. There is no way for a communicator to overcome this problem.

Feedback

A means of measurement—audience reaction—sales—polling

An Expanded Communication Model to Consider

In this model we have added S for source. All messages have a source. We have also added E for editing. All messages in the media go through an editing process. Feedback can come back to the sources and the editor as well as the communicator.

Source ——— Communicator ——— Editing ——— Audience

The Communicator's Task

1. Today, members of the mass media do more than record history, they help to shape it.

2. Mass communications work demands from its practitioners broad knowledge, sound judgment, quick decisions, and the realization that the words they write or speak may influence the lives of millions of people.

3. When you consider the problems in effective communication that we have discussed, it is a small wonder that there is criticism of the news media for the way they report events of major importance.

4. Reporting and commenting on the news is done by human beings who are subject to things like stored experience, but hopefully can be fair because of their training and experience.

5. Consider also that someone on every newspaper, radio, and TV station must decide which stories in the day's flow of events deserve the most prominent place in print or on the air.

6. Mass communications work is not always exciting because life is not always exciting. As in any business, there are hours of routine, often repetitious work. A solid, disciplined routine and a well-defined set of operating principles underlie everything.

7. Throughout the mass media, the challenge of social responsibility is felt by those at work. Frequently their judgment is tested under pressure in matters of taste, social restraint, and fairness, with few absolute rules to guide them.

8. Among the many opportunities enjoyed by the communicator, none is more important than the opportunity to help shape public opinion.

Definition of Mass Media (the Channel)

1. Printed word and picture
   a. the newspaper—news, opinion, entertainment, ads
   b. the magazine—news, features, entertainment, opinion, ads
   c. books—a longer range and more detailed examination of subjects, entertainment.
   d. pamphlets—direct mail, billboards—commercial and civic views.

2. Sound—radio—entertainment, news, opinion, and advertising

3. Sight and sound
   a. television—same as radio
   b. films—entertain but also may inform and persuade
   c. the Internet

4. There are several important agencies of communications adjacent to mass media.
   a. press associations
   b. feature syndicates
   c. advertising agencies
   d. ad departments of companies and institutions
   e. public relations counseling firms and publicity organizations
   f. research individuals and groups

Research

This is not a course in research, but students should realize that there is considerably more research going on in this field than was true fifty years ago. Much of the research from outside the media is to determine the impact of the media. How effective are the mass media in shaping thought (the cognitive aspect of mass communications)? In changing attitudes (the affective aspect of mass communications)? Or in moving people to action (the behavioral aspect of mass communications)? Scholars have been asking these questions for decades.

Agenda Setting

The press sets the agenda for its audience. It tells us what is important by its placement, i.e., banner headlines, leading off the 6 P.M. or 10 P.M. newscast. Most of us are lazy consumers. We don't read more than one newspaper or magazine. We don't look at more than one newscast. Consequently, the media can set our agenda.

Audience Research

Operators of the media desire to know the size and characteristics of their audiences. Newspapers and magazines can measure size by circulation figures. Radio and TV have to rely on ratings. Nielsen rates national TV programs while Arbitron rates local radio and TV stations. We will discuss how ratings work, and their impact, later.

Characteristics of the audience such as age, sex, income, racial heritage, household composition, and educational level are called **demographics**.

Use of Television Ratings

We will discuss this later, but it relates to measurement of the audience by firms such as Nielsen and Arbitron. The price a network charges for a 30-second commercial varies in prime-time shows, depending on their attractiveness to advertisers.

Advertising Research

Advertisers conduct research to try and identify what demographics are their best targets. Then they try to reach those demographics through the media.

2 Political, Economic and Social Importance of Mass Media

Theories of Press Freedom

Four basic theories of the press have emerged from the social and political environment of the past five centuries.

Authoritarian

This theory dates approximately from Henry VIII and the Reformation, during the 17th century when the functions of the press were clearly defined by the ruling class. Products of the presses—books as well as periodicals—were obliged to support the policies of government. Presses were privately owned, but they were licensed by the crown. This theory flourished for nearly 200 years, until the political revolt of 1688.

Libertarian

This theory arose during the l8th century, first in England, then in America. Yet, as early as 1644, John Milton pleaded for the abolition of government licensing of printed matter in his Areopagitica. John Locke in England and Thomas Jefferson in America became spokesmen for this theory. The press, under this concept, was to seek the truth "unfettered" by political authority.

Marxist

This theory is a 20th century development whereby the functions of mass media are determined by the political and economic philosophy of communism. Similar to the authoritarian theory, the press functions to maintain and extend the socialist system. All media are socialized. The state owns, directs, and operates the mass media for the "advancement of the existing order."

Social Responsibility

The hardest to define because it is still developing, this theory assumes that communicators, who enjoy a Constitutional freedom, have certain obligations to society.

Mainly, they should allow everyone to be heard. When the press is remiss under the libertarian theory, the public, through government or other agencies, must step in to guide it. Today in the United States it is very expensive to operate a newspaper, radio, or television station, so ownership is in the hands of a few. It is inherent, under this theory, that those few accept the responsibility of allowing all to be heard. If they don't, then the public has the right to force them to through the government.

Public Opinion

1. Our nation has become very public opinion-oriented.

2. We see polls every week that report how people feel about a given number of issues.

3. The media play a key role in the development of public opinion, as stated earlier.

4. Polling has become a significant form of feedback in our society. Our attention is directed daily at polls that measure public attitudes.

5. Allowing for a stated 3 to 4% of error, methodology has become sufficiently sophisticated that most reputable polls have an excellent record in forecasting winners of elections.

6. A sample of 1,600 adults can accurately reflect the opinions of 145 million if skilled polling scientists select the proper random sample.

1 *Political Process*

CANDIDATES FOR OFFICE

Candidates use the media to reach the public through:

    a. paid advertising that they control—election campaigns are now fought with 30-second sound bites rather than a discussion of issues.

    b. media coverage, which candidates, hopefully, do not control.

EXAMPLES

❶ The great TV debate of 1960 between Nixon and Kennedy—Kennedy's skillful use of the media.

❷ The return of Nixon in 1968, his skillful use of the media, and his refusal to debate McGovern in 1972.

❸ The use of the media by Ronald Reagan. His debates with Carter, then Mondale.

❹ The 30-second attack commercials on TV in which candidates charge or insinuate that their opponents have done something stupid, illegal, unethical, or immoral.

❺ George Bush's heavy and successful use of such tactics against Michael Dukakis.

❻ The way Bill Clinton presented himself as a "New Democrat" and made George Bush eat his "read my lips" pledge from the previous campaign.

THE WATCHDOG CONCEPT

The news media have a vital role to play in a democracy—that of "watchdog" over the government, searching out fraud and corruption at all levels (city, state, and national).

THE MARKETPLACE CONCEPT

The media also serves as a "marketplace" of ideas and information. The aims and policies of government are discussed extensively by opposition political leaders, commentators, editors, and the public in general through the nation's news media.

THE GATEKEEPER FUNCTION

On every medium that transmits news, some individual must perform what is called the "gatekeeper" function; that is, they must decide whether or not to use the item and what emphasis to give to it. This function begins with the news gatherer, moves through several editorial stages, and finally rests in the hands of the consumer.

② Economic Fabric

1. Mass media play a major role in the business life of the nation. This occurs principally through advertising in newspapers, magazines, radio, and TV.

2. So firmly integrated are the media with the economic well-being and growth of the nation that the survival of a free enterprise system is almost unthinkable without advertising.

3. The media's coverage of economic news also has an impact on our economy, i.e., strikes, economic indicator reports, the stock market, and general business developments.

4. The business community holds a popular misconception that the news media are out to get corporations. The media refute this charge, claiming that they are only after the truth and have no desire to destroy others.

③ Social Structure

1. News about the way we behave, our tastes, our work habits, religious beliefs, customers, dress, ideas regarding sex, etc. have great impact. We are a nation of imitators.

2. Television probably has the great impact on change because it is dramatic and personal.

3. The coverage of protest and violence has had pronounced impact and has stirred great debate.

4. By reflecting the values and interest of society the media have influenced great social change in this country, most noticeably in the area of civil rights and civil liberties.

EXAMPLE The Condom Controversy

❶ The controversy over airing commercials for birth control devices, specifically condoms. Several Surgeon Generals urge the use of condoms as the best protection against the AIDS infection right now, barring abstinence.

❷ Networks have refused to carry condom advertising for fear that such commercials would offend large segments of their audiences.

❸ Planned Parenthood criticizes this by saying that TV carries programs and commercials promoting sexuality while turning down birth control ads.

❹ Thus you have two powerful social forces opposing each other and the networks are caught in the middle.

3 Freedom of the Press

Responsibility versus Performance

1. The Constitution guarantees freedom of the press but it does not define it. A definition has been framed over 200 plus years by laws, court decisions, and common practice.

2. Despite its excesses and limitations, our press system is vastly preferable to any other system in the world.

3. In general the trend is toward less and less legal restriction on what can be printed and spoken. This increased freedom adds to the social responsibility of the communicator.

Newspapers and Magazines

1. William Caxton set up the first press in England in 1476. But not until 1694, more than 200 years later, did the printers enjoy freedom to print for the people.

2. As discussed earlier, authoritarianism meant licensing—or censorship before a printer had a chance to print. Thus, unauthorized printing was a crime.

3. Henry VIII was regarded as the instigator of prior restraint. In 1534, he proclaimed that all printers must have royal permission to set up business.

4. Prior restraint lasted until the late 1600s—then died although severe sedition and libel laws were passed.

5. Prior restraint lingered on in the colonies. On September 25, 1690, Benjamin Harris issued Public Occurances, Both Foreign and Domestic. It was his first issue and also his last, because he neglected to obtain a royal license.

6. The United States Constitution and subsequent Bill of Rights basically provided the freedom to print, and it gradually became an accepted principle in America.

7. Traditionally, the American judicial interpretation is that prior restraint violates press freedom. However, prior restraint did not die easily. First of all, courts

have ruled that freedom of the press is not absolute—there are some limitations, Secondly, the Constitution was national law, and sometimes state law was different.

8. *Near v. Minnesota,* 1931—This became the bedrock case for all future cases involving prior restraint. It was the first time that the press guarantees of the First Amendment were applied to the states, through the due process clause of the Fourteenth Amendment. Near published a weekly newspaper in Minneapolis and criticized local officials of conspiracy with racketeers. A Minnesota state court forbade the newspaper to publish "scandalous" articles under a Minnesota state law called the Minnesota Gag Law. This decision was reversed by the Supreme Court. The Court ruled that this was prior restraint, unconstitutional under the First Amendment, and, in doing so, tied the First Amendment to the Fourteenth. This was a great boost to press freedom.

9. *Esquire v. U.S.,* 1943—In 1943, the Postmaster General proposed to withdraw use of the second-class mailing rate from *Esquire* magazine because he felt that Esquire was "not contributing to the public welfare," one of the requirements necessary to obtain a second-class permit. Esquire, at that time, was the *Playboy* of the 1940s. The publishers carried the case to the Supreme Court in 1946, where the court upheld a decision by the U.S. Court of Appeals that the Postmaster General was in error. This decision basically told the federal government and its officials to leave matters like this to the courts.

10. *Pentagon Papers Case,* 1971—Another test of prior censorship came in the summer of 1971, when the government won a temporary restraining order prohibiting the New York Times from continuing a series summarizing the "top secret" 7,000 page, 48-volume "History of the U.S Decision Making Process on Vietnam Policy." This has been referred to as the Pentagon Papers case. The Supreme Court granted the Nixon administration a temporary restraining order barring the *Times* and the *Washington Post* from publishing the stories which had first been granted by a lower court. This was a shocking setback for the press and represented the first time in the history of the country that the executive branch had been successful in involving prior restraint upon the press. Ultimately, the court ruled in a 6-3 vote that the government had failed to show that national security was being endangered by the further publication of these papers.

Broadcasting

1. Radio and TV are licensed to broadcast by the FCC under the concept that broadcasting is in the public domain. The airways are public property, therefore the government has the right to regulate them for the benefit of the public. The FCC was not given the power to censor, but it has the power to renew or revoke license applications every seven years (it used to be every three years), so there is definitely an implied threat when it warns a station about a particular program or practice.

2. After World War I the government only allowed two frequencies on which a radio station could broadcast. With the growth of radio this became a major problem by the late 1920s. The Radio Act of 1927 was passed by Congress to eliminate chaos

among the growing number of broadcasters using the airwaves. A five-member Federal Radio Commission was given the authority to grant three-year licenses "in the public interest, convenience, or necessity" and "to provide fair, efficient and equitable service."

3. In 1934, legislation created the FCC and expanded membership to seven.

4. In 1941, the FCC ruled that a broadcaster "shall not be an advocate" in the Mayflower Broadcasting Co. decision. In 1949, it reversed its earlier decision ruling that a licensee could broadcast his/her own opinions on various subjects provided he/she gave opportunity for presentation of conflicting viewpoints (fairness). In 1970, the FCC ruled that broadcasters who editorialize must invite specific spokesmen to state contrasting views. As a result of this decision, broadcasters editorialized less than 50% on a regular basis and many with caution of subject matter. In 1987, the FCC dropped the Fairness Doctrine and Congress dropped a rider to an appropriations bill that would have reinstated it under the threat of a presidential veto. But it is not yet a dead issue.

5. *The Red Lion Decision*—In 1969, the Supreme Court backed the authority of the FCC when it ruled that no station owner can monopolize a frequency to the exclusion of fellow citizens—that a license permits broadcasting, but not exclusive broadcasting.

Media Criticism

1. When authoritarianism faded in England, sedition laws took its place. Sedition laws made it a crime to criticize the government.

2. *Truth as a Defense*—Journalists first had to establish the principle of truth as a defense against charges of sedition or criminal libel.

3. *The Zenger Case*—John Peter Zenger was an immigrant printer who printed a colonial paper, the *New York Journal,* for a group of middle class businessmen. The writers in the paper constantly attacked and criticized the colonial governor, William Cosby. Cosby finally had Zenger jailed on charges of seditious libel. The businessmen hired Andrew Hamilton, a famed colonial attorney, to defend him. Hamilton argued truth as a defense and also argued that the jury had the right to decide not only the fact (that the libel had been printed) but the law (punishment). This was in 1735 and both arguments were contrary to English law at the time. The English tradition was that the greater the truth, the greater the libel. The jury decided the fact, the judge decided the law. Zenger was acquitted thanks to the emotion created by Hamilton. The verdict did not change the law at that time, in that it was 70 more years before a New York state legislature wrote into its books that a jury could decide both fact and law and that truth could be used as defense of libel. The Zenger decision did make criticism of public officials respectable—thus opening up regular criticism of the government by colonial editors, which moved us closer to the Revolutionary War.

4. *Federalist v. Republican Press*—after the war we had a highly partisan press, as we shall see when we discuss press history. Newspapers generally lined up along conservative and liberal lines, and criticism was low-level on both sides.

5. *Alien and Sedition Acts*—As a reaction to this criticism, the John Adams administration had the Alien and Sedition Acts passed in 1798. They were used to suppress criticism of the Federalist-controlled government, but they backfired when public unhappiness over their administration resulted in the election of Thomas Jefferson in 1800. The acts were then allowed to expire.

6. *Wartime Censorship*—In reporting war, how do you report the news and not give information that would aid the enemy? The problem was poorly handled in the Civil War but vastly improved upon during the First and Second World Wars. In both situations, the government the government hired veteran newspapermen to head bureaus working with the press in releasing information and asking for voluntary compliance in certain areas of security-type information.

7. However, the Espionage Act of 1917, and the Trading With the Enemy Act and the Sedition Act of 1918, did widen government censorship and set a precedent for national emergencies. The Espionage Act gave the Post Office the authority to bar periodicals from the mails and the Sedition Act made it a crime to write or publish any disloyal, profane, scurrilous or abusive language about the federal government.

8. *Schenck v. U.S.*, 1919—produced the "clear and present danger" theory, as espoused by Justice Oliver Wendell Holmes. Schenck urged draft resistance in a pamphlet. He was convicted of violating the Espionage Act. Holmes said, and the court agreed, that under certain circumstances restrictions on what people may say and write are justifiable. Truth is not suppressed, but in cases of "clear and present danger" the democratic process for finding truth is too slow. Therefore, if a "clear and present danger" exists, one's First Amendment rights can be restricted.

Restrictions on Reporting

1. Surprisingly, this right is not as much protected by law and legal precedent as the right to print and to criticize. It concerns the right of access to news. No one can be compelled to talk to a reporter.

2. Congress has seldom conducted its business in private since 1842, but legislative committees and state and local governing bodies often hold "executive sessions" to transact the public's business privately. Committee access is left up to the willingness of the chairman and members.

3. In the courtroom, reporters are subject to the rules and procedures set down by the presiding judge. Reporters have no automatic right of attendance. Photographers and TV-radio reporters have had only limited success in covering trials with cameras or microphones.

4. In courtrooms, reporters are protected from libel damages when reporting on testimony because it is considered public record. This is called the doctrine of qualified privilege. However, the reports must report testimony accurately to avoid problems.

5. The right to access to reports is a big problem on the local level, i.e., boards of education, city councils, county boards.

6. By 1975, most all states (but not Texas) had some form of open meeting law as well as laws guaranteeing the opening of public records to reporters needing access to them.

7. The most publicized denial of access to news has been in the national executive departments—for national defense reasons.

8. Freedom of Information Acts in 1966 and 1974 gave citizens legal recourse against arbitrary withholding of information by a federal agency. The 1974 amendment was passed over President Ford's veto and narrowed the scope of exemption that protected certain categories of government files from public disclosure, such as secrets that affect the national security.

9. In 1980, Congress passed a bill exempting most consumer information from being disclosed by the FTC.

10. The Reagan administration has campaigned to give substantial or total exemption from the act to the CIA and FBI. In 1986, Congress finally passed a bill giving federal law-enforcement agencies new authority to withhold documents.

11. This battle has gone in cycles. The Reagan administration has generally moved to restrict the free flow of certain information related to law enforcement, national security, defense, etc.

12. In 1977, the Government in the Sunshine Law required more than 50 federal boards and agencies with two or more members to conduct most meetings in the open.

Reporter's Confidentiality

1. In 1972 the Supreme Court, by a 5-4 vote, decided that news reporters have no special immunity under the First Amendment not to respond to grand jury subpoenas and provide information about their sources. (Caldwell case).

2. The court recognized the problem of news sources drying up if reporters could not promise immunity, so they left the door open for Congress to enact legislation binding on federal courts and grand juries.

3. They also invited state legislatures to enact "shield" laws, saying that the court would be powerless to bar such legislation.

4. Shield laws have been enacted in a number of states but they vary from state to state.

5. One of the most publicized cases was that of William Farr, a Los Angeles reporter, who, during the mid-1970s, served 46 days in jail for protecting sources for a story about the Charles Manson murder trial.

6. In 1980, California voters enacted a state constitutional amendment that included the exact language of the state's shield law.

Police Raids of Newsrooms

Countless subpoenas have been issued in both criminal and civil cases over this matter and police, in various parts of the country, have carried out raids of newsrooms searching for information. This led to the enactment of the Privacy Protection Act in 1980 that requires authorities to request voluntary compliance or to use subpoenas with advance notice and the opportunity for a court hearing rather than search warrants when they seek reporters' notes, films, etc.

Seizure of Telephone Records

In 1973, it was disclosed that Nixon administration officials had secretly subpoenaed both office and home telephone call records of columnist Jack Anderson and the bureau chiefs of several news organizations. In 1979 the Supreme Court refused to hear the case, leaving unanswered the question of how reporters could protect themselves against these seizures.

Reporters in the Courtroom

1. In 1976 a trial judge in a Nebraska murder trial entered an order restraining the news media from reporting the existence of any confession or admission made by the defendant until the trial jury had been impaneled.

2. The Supreme Court overruled the judge in this case, stating that the press was entitled to report all evidence presented. By that time the case was over. Chief Justice Burger, in overruling the judge, made it clear the ruling did not prevent future "gag" orders.

3. Great fears were raised in 1979 when the court ruled that members of the public have no constitutional rights to attend criminal trials. They reversed themselves in 1980, ruling that the public has a constitutional right to attend criminal trials even when defendants want to exclude them.

4. Prior to that reversal there had been 160 successful closings of courtrooms to public and press—126 pretrial hearings and 34 trials.

5. The gap was closed in 1986 when the court ruled in a 7-2 decision that the public has a First Amendment right to attend pretrial hearings in criminal cases over the objections of defendants.

6. The bottom line is simple. If a reporter does not have access, he or she does not have the right to print.

Cameras in the Courtroom

The United States Supreme Court ruled in 1981 that states have the right to allow TV, radio, and photographic coverage of criminal trials. In 1992, all but six states and DC permitted cameras in their courtrooms.

Libel and Slander

1. Defamation is language that injures a person's reputation, embarrasses them, or holds them up to ridicule.

2. *Hate Speech:* In 1992, the Supreme Court ruled that the First Amendment prohibits the government from "silencing speech on the basis of its content."

Legislatures may not single out racial, religious or sexual insults as "hate speech" or bias crimes.

This decision likely invalidates many of the speech codes adopted at public universities; under such codes, students face punishment for insults or harassment on the basis of race, religion or sex.

3. Before a plaintiff can expect to win a libel suit, he or she must establish at the outset that:
   - The offending statement has been published.
   - The plaintiff or person bringing the action has been identified in the statements.
   - The statement is defamatory.
   - It appeared because the defendant—the one being sued, in this case the publication or broadcaster—was somehow at fault.

4. *Defenses:*
   - Truth
   - Privilege
   - Fair Comment and Criticism—A major defense of libel has emerged over the years in this country. It is called fair comment and criticism and, as the result of court decisions, has framed a shield behind which the press can be protected for commenting on and criticizing the acts of:
     a. public officials—the groundwork was laid in the *Zenger* case but it was officially put in the records in 1808.
     b. public figures—first recognized in the *Walker v. AP* case in 1967
     c. private citizens who get involved in public issues—first recognized in the *Rosenbloom v. Metromedia* case in 1971, then modified by the *Gertz* case in 1974.

5. *The Sullivan Ruling*—In its March 29, 1960 edition, the *New York Times* printed a full page ad requesting contributions for the civil rights movement in the South and for the legal defense of Dr. Martin Luther King, Jr. The ad was placed by a N.Y. public relations firm and signed for by 20 clergymen. L. B. Sullivan, a Montgomery, Alabama, city commissioner, sued the Times for libel because of claimed inaccurate statements. Alabama courts awarded Sullivan $500,000 damages, but the Supreme Court reversed the decision and said that only when errors are made with malice, with knowledge that they are errors, or with reckless disregard for accuracy—does the fair comment defense collapse in an action brought by a public official or a public figure. This was 1964. (*Butts* case)

6. *Private Citizens*—In 1971, the Supreme Court, in *Rosenbloom v. Metromedia*, extended the *Sullivan* ruling to include a private person involved in an event of public interest. However, in *Gertz v. Welch*, in 1974, the court modified this position. It ruled that such a person might recover damages by proving that the media were guilty of negligence.

7. *Public Figures v. Private Citizens*—There is sometimes a fine line between who is a public figure and who is a private citizen. When does a private citizen become a public figure? The media have to be careful about this concept and the courts usually have the last say in such matters.

8. *Firestone v. Time, Inc.,* 1976—In 1976 Mary Alice Firestone and her husband, Russell Firestone III of the Firestone Tire and Rubber Company, divorced. The divorce was widely publicized and Mrs. Firestone talked to the press every day after the proceedings. Later the Supreme Court ruled that Mrs. Firestone was not a public figure and she won a $100,000 libel judgment against *Time* magazine for incorrectly reporting that Mr. Firestone had been granted a divorce from her on grounds of extreme cruelty and adultery. *Time's* attorney's argued that she was a public figure and had to prove malice or reckless disregard for the truth.

9. In 1979, Chief Justice Warren Burger commented in *Hutchinson v. Proxmire* that he had doubts about the so-called rule of summary judgment on First Amendment grounds. He stated that the proof of actual malice calls a defendant's state of mind into question and does not readily lend itself to summary judgment. This means that just because a person is a public figure, the court will not give a summary judgment to the publisher until the merits of the case are heard.

10. *Carol Burnett v. National Enquirer,* 1981—Ms. Burnett sued the publication because in March 1976, it published a report she claimed made her appear drunk and rowdy in a fashionable Washington, D. C. restaurant. The item was incorrect, the *Enquirer* subsequently admitted, and it ran a correction apologizing for any "embarrassment" to the entertainer. The jury agreed that the *Enquirer* published its item with "reckless disregard for the truth"—what a public figure must prove to win a libel case. They awarded her $1.6 million general and $1.3 million punitive damages.

11. *Sharon v. Time,* 1985—Ariel Sharon, Israel's defense minister, sued *Time* for $50 million. He accused the magazine of erroneously linking him to a massacre of 700 Arabs in a Lebanese refugee camp. He lost his suit because he could not prove Time had acted in malice and had known the story to be false or had serious doubts about its truth. He was able to prove that Time had committed errors, and that the reporter was negligent.

12. *Westmoreland v. CBS*—General William Westmoreland sued CBS for $120 million in 1985 for accusing him of lying during the Tet offensive of the Vietnam war. He withdrew his suit after 18 months and, under an agreement between CBS and the general, both sides paid their own legal costs, and CBS made no apology or retraction.

13. In 1986, the Supreme Court justices widened the scope of the *Sullivan* standard in several rulings.

   ■ They ruled that a public-figure libel plaintiff must demonstrate "actual malice" by clear and convincing evidence" to overcome a defendant's motion that a summary judgment dismissing the suit be granted by the trial judge.
   ■ They then ruled that the states may not place the burden on media libel defendants to prove truth in suits brought by private figures if they involve coverage of issues of public concern. The private figure must prove, not just claim, that the news account was false.

Right of Privacy

1. No one has to talk to the press.

2. Public officials and public figures give up a good deal of their right to privacy.

3. The key case in the right of privacy is *Hill v. Time, Inc.,* 1952

    a. *Hill v. Time, Inc.*— In 1952, three escaped convicts held James Hill, his wife, and five children hostage in their suburban Philadelphia home. After the ordeal, Hill refused to grant interviews and moved his family to Connecticut. A year and a half later, *The Desperate Hours* was published as a novel and later adapted for the Broadway stage. Then it became a movie. *Life* magazine published an article about the play and used pictures of the Hills' former home. Headline read: "True Crime Inspires Tense Play." Hill sued for invasion of privacy and won. He won the appeal, but later the Supreme Court ruled that newsworthiness will override an individual's right to privacy.

4. In 1975, the Supreme Court struck down a Georgia law that made it a misdemeanor to print or broadcast the name of a rape victim. Despite this rather complex ruling, broadcasters and newspapers still use great caution in disclosing the names of rape victims.

The Privacy Act of 1974

1. This law stipulated types of information about individuals that could not be disclosed by federal agencies, and provided means whereby persons could determine the nature of information about themselves in official files.

2. Most colleges and universities will not release confidential information about students, citing the Buckley Amendment of 1974 to the federal Family Education and privacy Rights Act.

PRIVACY CAN BE VIOLATED IN THE FOLLOWING WAYS:

- Unreasonable intrusion upon one's physical solitude.
- Unauthorized appropriation of a person's name or likeness for commercial purposes.
- Unreasonably placing an individual in a false light before the public.
- Unjustified publication of embarrassing facts.

Obscenity and Pornography

1. The Supreme Court has always had a difficult time of drawing firm legal lines as to what is obscene and what is not. ("I know it when I see it.")

2. The court has maintained that certain materials are not protected by the First Amendment and that the government can suppress these materials.

3. In 1957, the court ruled that the standard for judging obscenity is "whether, to the average person, applying contemporary standards, the dominant theme of the material, taken as a whole, appeals to the prurient (pur-e-ant—craving restlessly) interest."

4. The court ruled that the portrayal of sex is not itself sufficient reason to deny protection—obscenity and sex are not synonymous.

5. In 1966, the Court set forth a new definition. Three elements must come together:
   a. that the dominant theme of the material taken as a whole appeals to a prurient interest in sex.
   b. the material is patently offensive because it affronts contemporary standards relating to the description or representation of sexual matters.
   c. the material is utterly without redeeming social value.

6. In 1973 (*Miller v. California*), in a 5-4 vote, the court revised this definition to say:
   a. Whether the average person, applying contemporary community standards, would find the work taken as a whole appealing to the prurient interest.
   b. Whether the work depicts or describes in a patently offensive way sexual conduct specifically defined by the applicable state law.
   c. Whether the work taken as a whole lacks serious literary, artistic, political, or scientific value.

7. Community standards were defined in 1974. They may be those of the state but do not necessarily have to be representative of any specific geographical boundary. The court also ruled that nudity alone is not obscene and prohibitions apply only to public portrayal of hardcore sex.

8. As a result of these decisions, the legislatures of almost every state have set about reviewing their own obscenity laws.

UNIT I: STUDY GUIDE

1. Define each of the following:

    a. communication
    b. mass communication
    c. journalist
    d. "The Press"

2. Describe the communication process by:

    a. defining the four aspects of the process
    b. describe four limitations of the process
    c. describing how those limitations can be overcome
    d. how the communicator determines effectiveness

3. Discuss the watchdog, marketplace and gate keeping functions of the press.

4. Define the following theories of the Press:

    a. Authoritarian
    b. Marxist
    c. Libertarian
    d. Social Responsibility

5. Briefly describe the impact of media in (a) our political process (b) our economic fabric and (c) social change.

6. Describe how scientific polling is done today.

7. What does convergence mean?

8. Define Freedom of the Press.

9. When did the right to print become an accepted principle in America?

10. What was the importance of the *Near v. Minnesota* decision?

11. What did the Pentagon papers case represent?

12. Discuss the significance of the *Zenger* decision.

13. What four things does a plaintiff have to prove in a libel case?

14. What is meant by fair comment and criticism? (Be sure to include in this discussion what happens when errors are made in commenting and criticizing, i.e., *Sullivan* decision.)

15. In the *Sharon* trial, the former defense minister of Israel, lost because he could not prove what critical point?

16. Is the right to print and criticize absolute? Why or why not?

17. Essentially, what is basic in the right to report?

18. Discuss the confidentiality issue as it pertains to federal courts and state courts.

19. List the Supreme Court's 1973 definitions of obscenity.

UNIT I: REVIEW QUESTIONS

- What was the opening statement I gave you regarding our discussion on scope?

  Newspapers etc. are large in scope

- Radio, TV and newspapers: How many dailies? How many weeklies?

  mor weeklies than dailies

- How many periodicals? How many general interest?

  30,000   600

- Which has the biggest audience—AM or FM radio?

  FM radio 70%

- How many homes in America have TV sets?

  99%

- How many homes wired for cable? What percentage?

  66% +20% for satellite

- Average family watches TV?

  7 hours a day

- Define communication.

  transmission of ideas attitudes

- What is interpersonal communication? Intrapersonal communication?

  group comm.   self. comm.

- Define mass communication.

  communication to large and diverse audiences

- Name the four basic elements of the communication process (include technical names).
  Communicator/incoder—message—channel-audience (decoder) -- ˈ

- Name and define four limitations and how they might be overcome.
  channel noise (static-distractions)—redundancy
  semantic noise (word understandings)—clearly defining audience (use simple words)
  stored experience (frame of reference)—research *- values*
  dissonance (inconsistent)

- The average daily newspaper is written for an 8th-grade vocabulary.

- How do you measure effectiveness—feedback? from audience to communicator—examples

  Random samples with 3% error
  spontaneous feedback

- In the expanded model all communication begins with a __Source__?

- What is meant by "E"? Who judges?

  Editor / Gatekeeping process

- Why is there so much criticism of the news media?

  because of the human aspect

- Who does the term "the press" apply to?

  anyone who gathers and spreads news info

- What is the agenda-setting theory? What would another term be for it? (gatekeeping)

  media sets public agenda with headlines

- What is mean by communicator research?

  Study of successful communicators

- A sample of __1,600__ can reflect the opinions of __145 mill__?

- How do candidates for public office communicate with the public? advertising and coverage

- How do political leaders learn what people think? Feedback

  commission polls

- Do people always vote based on the platforms and substance of the candidates?

  No

- What do we mean by a trial balloon? a leak?

  purposly leak info to see reactions

- Define the watchdog concept, the marketplace concept, and the gatekeeper concept.

  the media should inform the public over the News of Gov.

- Would it be possible to have the free society we enjoy without a free press?

  True

- How has advertising affected our standard of living?

  stimulates free enterprise

- Can public opinion influence public officials?

  generally yes

- How does the media influence our habits?

  we imitate what we see and hear

- Define the four theories of the press.
  Authoritarian—use of a license
  Libertarian—all people have access to public express—unbothered by government
  Marxist—government owned
  Social Responsibility—open marketplace of ideas—government agency to enforce

- Is social responsibility controversial? Why?

  Yes it is subjective

- Define freedom of the press.

  You are free to write or say anything you please

- Where do we get it? What does it say about responsibility?

  First amendment. Nothing

- Define prior restraint before a message can be transmitted—licensing.

  restraining a message

- What replaced licensing laws? (sedition laws)

  sedition law — can't criticize government

- Did freedom to print exist from the beginning in the American colonies?

  No, Authoritarianism

- Is the First Amendment absolute?

  No not in times of war or security

- What happened in the *Near v. Minnesota* case?

  Supreme court ruled a gag order was uncostitutional

- What was unique about the *Pentagon Papers* case?

  First time that Exec. branch used prior restraint on Media

- Why do broadcasters complain that they do not enjoy the same First Amendment rights as publishers?

  Because of FCC

- What was the Fairness Doctrine?

  must allow opposition to respond in debates

- What was the *Red Lion* decision?

  Supreme court ruled FCC right to regulate

- What is mean by "the greater the truth the greater the libel"?

  If truth is proven then you are guilty

- What did the *Zenger* decision do? (1) raised the question (2) made criticism respectable

  He got off. It raised issue of truth as liable. Made criticism respectable

- What did the Alien & Sedition Acts do? Why were they passed?

  Alien — deportation
  sedition — illegal to criticize gov.

- What is the legal status of the right to report?

  Not as clearly defined

- Who has to talk to a reporter?

  Nobody

- Can reporters be excluded from congressional committee meetings? court sessions?

  Yes if National security / Judges can hold out Media

- Where is the right to report most often denied?

  The local level

- Can a newspaper publish a defamatory statement made during a court trial?

  Yes if they get it correct

- What is the status of open meetings and open records laws in the states?

  it is illegal

- What was the purpose of the Freedom of Information Acts? people's right to know

  Protected public's right to records on self

- What type of protection do reporters have not to reveal sources? (discuss shield laws)

  None in federal court   In state court shield law

- Can law enforcement agencies raid newsrooms?

  Yes but they give advance Notice

- Can reporters attend pre-trial hearing over the objections of defendants?

  Yes

- What does libel damage? (reputation)

  defamation

- What does a plaintiff have to prove in a libel case? (identification and publications, defamation, fault)

  malice wr

- What is fair comment and criticism?

  Protects press when they criticize officials or public figures

- Who does it apply to? public officials (long standing)? public figures? private citizens?

- What did the *New York Times* decision do? (it created a new freedom from libel) reckless disregard or libel

  prove malice or reckless disregard of Truth

- What does a private citizen have to prove?

  Negligence

- What was the result of the *Carol Burnett v. National Enquirer* case?

  Burnett proved disregard of truth she won

- Explain the 1973 Supreme Court's ruling regarding the test for pornography.

  1. work taken as a whole appeals to sex
  2.
  3. lacks serious artistic political scientific value

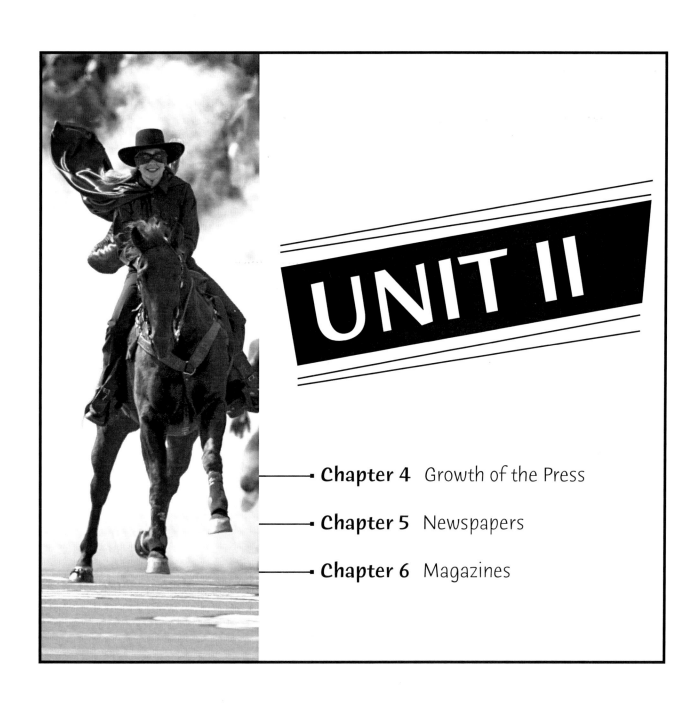

UNIT II

• **Chapter 4** Growth of the Press

• **Chapter 5** Newspapers

• **Chapter 6** Magazines

Growth of the Press

The Colonial Press

1. The first newspaper publishers were primarily printers, not editors.

2. Benjamin Harris published *Publick Occurrences, Both Foreign and Domestic* in 1690 as a journalistic effort, but he only brought out one issue because he published without a license.

3. James Franklin, in the *New England Courant,* gave Boston readers of the 1720s the first readable and exciting American newspaper. He also ran into trouble because he published news that "offended" the colonial governor. He was jailed as a result.

4. Ben Franklin really was the first editor to lend respectability to journalism with his *Pennsylvania Gazette.* He made money on advertising. He was a crusader for progress, but knew how far he could go without causing trouble with the authorities.

5. Usually, the paper nearest to the scene of an event covered it; others copied the report or relied upon official announcements or messages.

6. As the Tory-Patriot conflict developed many newspaper editors became political pamphleteers. By 1750, the newspaper was the channel of information and interpretation on hotly debated issues.
   a. James Rivington of New York led the Tory Press
   b. John Dickinson of Pennsylvania led the Whig Press
   c. Sam Adams was the radical or patriot leader

The Revolutionary Press

1. The press fanned the flame of revolution and served as the motivator.

2. Tom Paine's work *Common Sense* sold 12,000 copies in three months in the spring of 1776. His *Crisis* papers soon followed to spur the patriot cause.

3. Another leading spokesman for the patriot cause was Isaiah Thomas. On the masthead of his newspaper, *The Massachutts Spy,* he had a snake, cut into 13 parts with a slogan "Join or Die."

4. At the end of the Revolution:
   a. newspapers were established as being able to influence masses.
   b. there were more newspapers and more readers.
   c. there was some typographical design and headlines.
   d. precedents for press freedom had been established.

Press of the New Republic

1. The role of the press in this period was to work for organization, ratification of the Constitution following the failure of the Articles of Confederation.

2. The Federalist Papers by Alexander Hamilton.

The Party Press, 1783–1800

1. Partisan journalism was still the rule of the day as the country developed.

2. Federalists—led by Hamilton, favored a strong central government.

3. Anti-Federalists—led by Thomas Jefferson, favored independent states' rights

4. Editorial attacks were often vicious and libelous and filled news columns on partisan views. This finally brought about the Alien & Sedition Acts.

5. Frontier papers soon found their own champion, however, in Andrew Jackson and the Democratic Party. Western papers were highly partisan and freewheeling.

6. Magazines were few during this period, but between 1800 and 1840 several hundred quarterly, monthly, and weekly magazine ventures sprang up.

7. Popular journalism was under way by the 1830s. The U.S. had more newspapers (over 1,200) with a greater reading audience than any country in the world.

The Penny Press (6 cents to 1 cent)

1. In the 1830s, a low-priced newspaper emerged that was edited for the masses. It appealed to the common man and depended on a large circulation to attract profitable advertising.

2. Benjamin Day's *New York Sun,* first of the penny papers in 1833, had a circulation of more than 20,000 by 1837, the largest in the world.

3. "News, not views" was the credo of James Gordon Bennett, who founded the *New York Herald* in 1835. He added some substance to his newspaper and began to gather news. He refined techniques for reporting the news and hired reporters to cover the city.

4. Horace Greeley edited the *New York Tribune* in 1841 and began to give an independent voice to the editorial page. He rejected many principles of his party and attempted to be socially responsible. Greeley's paper appealed to the common man.

5. Still another leader was Henry J. Raymond, who started the *New York Times* in 1851 and concentrated on foreign coverage, sound editorial policy, and in-depth reporting.

6. This period saw the newsgathering and reporting functions come into their own.

7. It also saw the opinion function grow distinct from the news function.

8. Finally, in order to sell papers there was sensationalism and human interest emphasizing a localization of news.

The Personal Press

1. Out of the penny press came a group of editors whose personalities dominated the newspaper. Readers identified with the individual rather than the paper.

2. Horace Greeley was definitely in this class, but others included
   a. William Cullen Bryant of the *New York Post*
   b. Samuel Bowles II of the *Springfield (Mass.) Republican*
   c. Joseph Medill of the *Chicago Tribune*

Partisanship Returns

1. Partisanship returned to journalism as the slavery issue began to divide the nation.

2. In 1827, Samuel Cornish, a Philadelphia Negro, founded the first Negro newspaper, *Freedom's Journal,* published in New York City.

3. *The Abolitionist Press* had been active for years, but became more effective in the 1840s and 1850s.

Development of Press Associations

1. The war with Mexico and the Civil War forced newspapers to expand their coverage.

2. Many newspapers sent correspondents to Texas to cover the war.

3. In 1848, six New York city papers formed the Associated Press of New York to cover the war for economy purposes.

The Civil War

1. The problem of censorship arose in the Civil War, which had as many first-hand accounts of battles than any war in our history. By the end of the war it was generally agreed that all dispatches from reporters had to be reviewed by a military provost.

2. Also, a new writing form emerged in the summary lead. In the summary leads that emerged, the reporter gives the who, what, when, where, why, and how. The basic point is that, instead of telling the story in narrative form, the reporter gives the most important information in the first paragraph.

New Journalism

1. In the 35 years between the close of the Civil War and the turn of the century the population of the country doubled, the national wealth quadrupled, and manufacturing production increased sevenfold.

2. A third of the population in 1900 was urban and 62% of the labor force was engaged in non-agricultural work.

3. Communication facilities expanded in this period. The federal postal service greatly extended free carrier service in the cities and instituted free rural delivery.

4. This was also the period where the tremendous increase in the circulation of the printed mass media which was the impetus for inventions such as the typewriter, the rotary press, the typesetting machine, photoengraving, color printing, etc.

5. Other journalistic developments included:
   a. the appearance of full-time reporters
   b. the establishment of news departments
   c. special education for careers in journalism

6. One of the giants of the profession emerged in this period. Joseph Pulitzer founded the *St. Louis Post-Dispatch* in 1878, bought the dying *New York World* in 1883. Within four years, it was the city's most successful paper. Pulitzer combined news with entertainment and sensationalism. He used bold headlines, color illustrations, and comics to attract and hold readers. He also insisted on comprehensive coverage, depth, and accuracy in news reporting.

7. Another leader emerged in William Randolph Hearst, whose *San Francisco Examiner* was a gift from his father in 1887. He bought the *New York Journal* in 1895 and went into competition with Pulitzer. He believed that news was a packaged commodity to be marketed like other consumer goods.

8. E. W. Scripps was the third of the giants. He built his newspapers in the smaller midwestern cities and appealed to the working class. He was a friend of the poor and ill-informed and was considered a "People's Champion."

9. These editors and others represented the new journalism. They were politically independent. They attacked business trusts and crusaded for many reforms.

Yellow Journalism

1. This period got its name from a cartoon strip named the "Yellow Kid."
2. It was personified by the circulation wars between Hearst and Pulitzer.
3. It reached its peak just prior to igniting the Spanish-American War.

Further Development of Press Associations

1. The Associated Press, started in 1848, was the only major news service in the early 1900s.
2. Scripps began the United Press in 1903.

3. Hearst, whose papers were denied AP membership, started International News Service in 1909.

4. UP and INS merged in 1958 to form UPI. AP is member-owned; UPI is privately owned.

The Opinion Magazines and Muckraking

1. Magazines also began to lower prices and appeal to mass audiences in the 1880s.

2. Leaders were *Ladies Home Journal, Saturday Evening Post, Colliers, McClures, Cosmopolitan,* and *Munseys.*

3. As was stated earlier, America experienced tremendous growth in the 1880s and 1890s—mostly unchecked. Big industry, big business, etc. grew unchecked. Big cities emerged as well as political machines—unchecked. Finally, around the turn of the century, journalists began to probe. It caused an explosion and Teddy Roosevelt referred to these writers as "muckrakers."

4. Ida M. Tarbell started it in *McClures* in 1903 with a "History of the Standard Oil Company." Others followed:
   a. Lincoln Steffens, *The Shame of the Cities.*
   b. David Graham Phillips, *The Treason of the Senate.* Also patent medicine.
   c. Upton Sinclair—*The Jungle.*

5. The magazines and newspapers hammered away against monopolies, corrupt politicians, patent medicine, and Wall Street. The movement lasted a little more than a decade.

The *New York Times*

1. During the period just before the First World War, Adolph Ochs built the *New York Times* into one of the world's greatest newspapers.

2. His slogan was "All the News that's Fit To Print" and he persisted in gathering and printing the news in all its varied aspects.

3. The coverage was extremely thorough. The papers published the texts of documents and speeches.

4. The newspaper followed a "dead pan" objective fashion of reporting as well as makeup.

Jazz Journalism—the 1920s

1. In the 1920s journalism reflected the period—"Return to Normalcy," prohibition, rise of organized crime, the jazz craze, prosperity, etc.

2. The rise of the tabloid newspaper came in the 1920s—along with the rise of sensationalism.
   a. *Illustrated Daily News*—catered to the lowest literate class with big pictures, screaming headlines, human interest stories, and sensational features. By 1924, it had attained the largest circulation of any newspaper in the country.

b. Hearst entered the *Daily Mirror* in 1924.

c. Bernard MacFadden's *Daily Graphic* "scarcely bothered to cover serious news at all."

3. The tabs gained recognition as sensational publications and, although their course has been much more moderate down through the years, they still emphasize photojournalism and still have the sensational connotation.

4. The period also saw the rise of the newspaper columnist—whose popularity rose to the degree of importance once enjoyed by the personal editor. The best-known names were David Lawrence, Mark Sullivan, Walter Lippmann, and Walter Winchell, later Drew Pearson.

5. Another journalistic development of the period was the news magazine.

a. Henry R. Luce founded *Time* in 1923 as a weekly that would summarize and departmentalize national and international news. Its objective was "fairness," not objectivity or impartiality,

b. *Newsweek* was established in 1933 and emulated Time's format.

c. *U.S. News and World Report* came in the early 1940s.

d. Luce brought out *Life* in 1936, a photojournalism effort, in competition with *Look*.

The New Deal

1. With the stock market crash and the election of Franklin D. Roosevelt in 1932 came a series of measures, regulations, and laws that represented an effort to get the country back on its feet again. It was called the New Deal.

2. It contained policies and programs related to agriculture, banking, and business, to name a few. It called for a degree of specialization on the part of the reporter who was going to try to interpret for his/her readers what was happening and how it was going to affect the country. Thus a marked degree of specialization never seen before became a characteristic of the daily newspaper, especially the large ones.

World War II

1. Many historians feel that the coverage of this war was the most impressive achievement the American press ever recorded.

2. Walter Cronkite first achieved some fame for his coverage of the Normandy Invasion. He parachuted behind enemy lines in advance of the invasion.

3. Ernie Pyle, who was killed in the war, became the best-known war correspondent. He won approval of his reading public not through analyzing, but by being close to the action and by telling the public what he saw.

4. Edward R. Murrow, whom we will talk about later, got his start with CBS Radio coverage of the developments that led to the war and then many notable reports during the war.

Korea and Vietnam

1. Both wars were unpopular—fought in remote place in difficult terrain and for causes only dimly understood by much of the American public.

2. The Korean conflict was a "police action" waged by the United Nations against North Korea, which had invaded South Korea.

3. There was initially no censorship and no pattern. When the war turned bad General MacArthur imposed rigid censorship policies.

4. We will talk more in depth later about Vietnam, which proved to be one of the most divisive events in our history.

5. Vietnam was our first televised war.

6. Many blamed the journalistic coverage of the war for the outcome, contending that sensational and biased coverage nurtured the antiwar movement and undermined the war effort.

7. It is interesting to note the changes made by our coverage in what it would allow the press to cover in subsequent battles, i.e., Grenada and the Mideast War. We will talk about this later.

The New Journalism of the 1960s and 1970s

1. According to Tom Wolfe, one of the so-called "new journalists," this movement began in the 1960s, when a number of writers found that they could stay in journalism and do everything the novelist had been able to do. Four techniques were employed:
   a. scene-by-scene construction of a story.
   b. extended realistic dialogue—you stay with someone long enough to get all kinds of dialogue that show his class background, his personality, his level of intelligence.
   c. use of point of view—describe the scenes through a character's pair of eyes.
   d. the use of status detail—describe clothing, furniture, interior decoration, hairstyles, mannerisms, behavior, etc.

2. The advocate style of journalism involved a small percentage of reporters who felt strongly about an issue and wrote their stories in such a way as to try to convince or influence their readers to feel the same way. This might involve distortion or fabrication, but they felt this was not a problem since their cause was right. The majority of working journalists rejected this style. To many it involves the old battle between objectivity and fairness. You can be honest and accurate—and fair without being objective. Objectivity is viewed by some as dull and dry data-process type reporting—uninteresting.

3. The third element was the rise of investigative reporting, which is still a strong element of journalism today.

The Underground Press

1. Another development in the 1960s that influenced the move to advocacy was the rise of the underground newspapers.

2. These newspapers and magazines rejected the traditional standards of objectivity, balance, and restraint in language.

3. They supported liberal political and social causes.

4. The more extreme were often libelous and intentionally crude.

5. The student press, to some degree on some campuses, got involved in this.

Recent History

1. Beginning in the 1960s, mounting costs forced a shakeout—mergers and newspaper closings typically left one city paper preeminent in the morning market and one in the evening.

2. The evening newspapers were then done in by television news.

3. Morning papers came to dominate and often eliminate their rivals.

4. The coming of chain ownership created a golden age of American journalism in large cities. Daily newspapers were not afraid to send reporters far and wide in pursuit of stories of corruption or of explaining the world.

5. The 1964 Sullivan ruling protected publishers even when they made errors if there was no malice or reckless disregard.

6. The Watergate story of the 1970s caused enrollments of journalism schools to grow.

7. At most big papers circulation, revenue, and profits grew through the 1970s, 1980s and into the 1990s.

8. But television began to make more inroads, especially cable TV.

9. In the 1990s came the digital networks and the Internet, unleashing forces that would ultimately undermine newspaper business models.

10. In response, newspapers sought to do three things: cut costs, diversify, and, above all, embrace the new technology.

11. These cutbacks and reductions fell heavily on foreign and investigative reporting.

12. Many newspapers began to experiment with online presentation, but they only copied closely what they were doing in print and didn't present new information.

13. A decisive blow may have been Google, with its powerful search engine that would either give you a quick answer to your question or refer you to a site that could, often a newspaper site.

14. While most newspapers remained profitable, concerns about the future caused the stock of most of the largest and prestigious newspapers to fall.

5 Newspapers

Introduction

1. The number of daily newspapers changed very little after World War II until the decade of 2000. From 1946 to 1970, the number of newspapers reached a high of 1,786 and a low of 1,570.

2. With the coming of the Internet newspapers have experienced a drop in readers and a drop in advertising. There are approximately 1,452 dailies with a circulation exceeding 52 million. Both figures are down from five years ago.

3. Fewer than a third of the daily newspapers have a circulation above 20,000 and about 115 exceed the 100,000 mark.

4. If there is an average American daily, it has a circulation of not more than 20,000 copies and serves a city of about 30,000.

5. A typical weekly has a circulation of about 4–5,000 copies.

6. Neither has much direct newspaper competition.

7. The most spectacular change has been the death of many of the so-called great newspapers in large cities such as Chicago, Philadelphia, Cleveland, and Washington. Closer to home we have seen mergers in Dallas, Houston, and San Antonio. The *Rocky Mountain News* in Denver folded in 2009. Also in 2009 *The Seattle Post-Intelligencer* decided to cease print publication and go completely online.

8. The major reasons for merger and consolidation have been the rising cost of production and competition from TV. Competition is now a factor in cities of more than 500,000 population.

9. TV news has replaced newspaper coverage in the minds of many Americans.

10. Total sales of newspapers have failed to keep pace with the nation's population growth.

11. In an age of lightning-fast electronic delivery of information, newspapers must find ways to supplement their traditional print delivery of news with electronic delivery methods.

Group Ownership in Print Media

1. There are more than 120 groups in the U.S. that own over 1,100 newspapers (75%).

2. A newspaper group is usually defined as two or more dailies in different markets under common ownership.

3. Largest of the groups in terms of properties is the Gannett Company, which owns 99 dailies, including *USA Today*, 8 TV stations, 16 radio stations, a magazine, a film production company, the Harris polling organization, and a billboard business.

4. Today, fewer than 20 American cities have fully independent competing dailies.

5. One of the major reasons why independent newspaper owners sell out to groups is to avoid inheritance taxes, which are so high at times that stockholders, often family members, have to sell their stock to pay the taxes. Group publishing corporations, whose stock is publicly owned, reduce their federal income taxes by using profits to purchase properties, and never face an inheritance tax problem.

6. But newspaper owners refute the criticism that one-newspaper cities are harmful:
   a. One strong newspaper in a city can often provide better news coverage and community service than two weaker ones.
   b. A strong newspaper may be more willing to attack entrenched and harmful interests in a city because it can absorb the financial retaliation aimed at it.
   c. Many conscientious editors and publishers, sensitive to being the only paper in town, go out of their way to provide fair and balanced coverage of the news.
   d. Newspapers do face heavy competition from radio and TV stations. This competition gives consumers more than one source of news and tends to keep everyone on their toes. This is referred to as media voices—separate ownerships of media seen, heard, and read in a community

7. Organizations and readers who do not want to hear the truth also at times exert extreme, unpleasant pressure against newspapers in revenge for stories they print. But the newspaper usually wins out because they are the only paper in town. Cite the feud between T. Boone Pickens and the *Amarillo Globe News*.

8. The *Fort Worth Star-Telegram* lost 1,200 subscribers and endured attacks from the Bell Helicopter Corporation, a hometown company, because it published articles disclosing a long-standing fault in the construction of Bell helicopters. This fault had contributed to the crashes in which about 250 servicemen died. A blue ribbon panel subsequently confirmed the newspaper's finding. The paper won a Pulitzer Prize for the series.

9. The *Lexington Herald-Leader* disclosed years-long illegal payments to University of Kentucky basketball players by school boosters and was attacked for "disloyalty" to the school. This involved bomb threats and angry petitions and lost subscribers totaling 369. This paper, too, won a Pulitzer.

10. The Newspaper Preservation Act was passed by Congress in 1970 after lively controversy. The act created exemptions in the antitrust law, so that two newspapers in the same town can combine all operations, except the newsroom.

What Do Readers Want?

1. Newspaper industry leaders discovered in the mid-1970s that readership was declining. It dropped 2 million between 1969 and 1975 while population rose during those years.

2. Editors and publishers conducted polls, seminars, and in-depth interviews and used other forms of public contact to find out what the problem was, what modern-day readers wanted, and how newspapers could satisfy those desires.

3. These studies showed that young people (21 to 35) and low-income minority groups felt little need for the newspapers in their daily lives. They had turned to TV for news.

4. Surveys also showed that many Americans criticized newspapers for:
   a. Political bias reflected in the news columns.
   b. Reporting that seemed to favor one side in a controversy over another.
   c. Attempts to cover up mistakes rather than admit and correct them.
   d. Influence from powerful outside pressure groups.
   e. Too much attention to bad news.
   f. Invasions of personal privacy.

5. As a result changes have been made in format and content. Magazine-type graphics have been used.

6. Today, only a few retain the format of eight narrow columns to a page. Instead, most use six wider columns arranged in modular style. Graphics experts are experimenting with other combinations of type, pictures, and color, seeking ways to make pages more eye-catching.

7. More stories about daily living problems have been emphasized.

8. More news summaries began to appear on the front page to compete with TV while more investigative reporting began to appear.

9. Enlarged special sections, usually weekly, have focused on fields of interest such as entertainment, sports, contemporary living styles, and finance.

10. Now, other critics maintained that newspapers have gone too far and have become too soft in hard news content.

11. While readership began to increase, as mentioned earlier, it has not kept pace with population growth in the country.

12. Changing lifestyles in the 1970s and 1980s seem to be accelerating. For example:
    - Time poverty—millions of adults work out, jog, ride bicycles and watch TV in the spare time.
    - Working women—women who are employed full or part-time—have increased since the 1950s from one-fourth to more than six out of 10. Many continue to be mothers and housewives, which leaves little time to read the newspaper.
    - Disaffection from conventional society among many persons in the lower socioeconomic groups in big cities, especially youths, has caused them to reject newspapers as irrelevant
    - The distressing amount of illiteracy and semiliteracy in the country limits the potential number of readers.

(**Functional illiteracy among American adults ranges from 20 to 30%—the inability to read a newspaper, understand the warnings on a bottle of medicine, or fill out a job application.**)

13. Today, readers want:
    - Better organization of their contents for quick reading.
    - Intensified coverage of personal topics such as health, finance, consumer news, parental problems, and do-it-yourself home projects.
    - Publication of more special-interest sections to reach diversified population groups.

A National Newspaper

1. The *Wall Street Journal* (2,069,463) and the Christian Science Monitor have traditionally been "national" newspapers, but restricted to specialized audiences. The Monitor has now ceased national distribution.

2. In 1982 the Gannett Company started *USA Today* and aimed it at a national general audience.

3. The contents are sent by satellite to 34 plants around the country for printing and distribution.

4. The newspaper has lost heavily. Gannett hoped it would reach profitability by 1988 but that did not happen until 1992. Current circulation is 2,284,219.

5. It has had a big impact with the abundant use of color and graphics.
    a. short main stories
    b. numerous capsulated summaries
    c. unusually detailed and up-to-the minute sports
    d. full-color weather page
    e. abundant use of color and graphics
    Many dailies have begun using four-color printing in the last decade.

6. The basic problem is that it can't attract classified and local retail advertising. Instead it has to compete for advertising dollars with national magazines and its ads cost more.

7. Also, about 20 percent of the paper's circulation are "bulk" sales; copies bought at a discount by hotels and airlines and given away.

R ole of Newspapers

The role of newspapers remains unchanged today despite the challenge of TV and the arrival of high-speed electronic newsgathering methods.

Primary

1. To inform
2. To comment and interpret (bring into focus)
3. To serve through advertising

Secondary

1. To campaign to desirable civic projects
2. To entertain through comics, cartoons, etc.
3. To serve as counselor, information bureau

Types of Newspapers

1. Weekly
2. Small Daily
3. Large Daily
4. Metropolitan Daily

General Organization

1. **Editorial**
   a. newsgathering—reporters under the direction of a news editor and/or city editor
   b. editing—copy desk, wire copy, layout
   c. photography
   d. editorial page under the direction of an editor
   e. graphics
2. **Advertising** (80% of Revenue)
   a. local display—sometimes called retail
   b. national—an individual coordinates with national advertising agencies and reps
   c. classified
   Today, chain stores have their own ads printed in multiple-page colored sections independently and then shipped to newspapers for insertion. This has had a big impact.
3. **Circulation**
   a. distribution
   b. promotion
4. **Production**
5. **Business**

Role of the Reporter

1. The majority of you who are thinking about majoring in journalism will probably begin your careers as a reporter.
2. Characteristics of reporters:
   a. 60% are men
   b. Minorities form only 5.6% of the work force
   c. Most have a college degree
   d. 25% have a journalism degree

3. What does a reporter do? Think of it this way. What happens in society? Babies are born. They grow up and go to school. They join clubs and organizations. They may be in athletics, or the band, etc. They graduate. Many go to college and repeat the process. If they don't they go into the work force. Many marry and have children of their own. They join organizations in the community and get involved in community affairs. Finally, they die. This is the way life is and this is what newspapers report day in and day out.

4. I say this to emphasize the fact that the job of a newspaper reporter is not terribly glamorous or terribly exciting—especially the beginner.

5. The big stories are few and far between.

6. Carl Bernstein and Bob Woodward have really glamorized reporting but their type of opportunity is once-in-a-lifetime.

7. Most of what a reporter does is routine.

8. A reporter, hopefully, grows better with experience. He or she becomes a better judge of what is news with time.

9. In considering what is news, reporters and editors have to consider:
   a. timeliness
   b. importance, to how many?
   c. interest

10. Factors that influence the selection of news
    a. deadlines
    b. competition
    c. convenience—cost, physical problems of getting the story. Researchers at Columbia Journalism Review found that in 1980 some 32 verbatim press releases published in a single edition of the *Wall Street Journal*. Some of these "news stories" even carried the "By Staff Writer" byline. It is easier and cheaper to publish the press release without making changes.
    d. bias—negative news—certain kinds of news.
    e. access—news that you can't get sometimes distorts the news.

11. We talked earlier about investigative reporting and I mentioned that more and more papers had hired investigative reporters. These are not rookies. They are skilled reporters with considerable background.

12. The public has grown somewhat cynical of investigative stories as a whole, so the newspaper that prints one wants it to be well done and effective. They normally don't just let anyone do one.

13. The feeling is that a reporter is going to have some bias—but that they can attempt to be fair in their coverage.

14. This calls for dedication—it also requires some background and experience.

Newspaper Organization

- Morgue—clippings of stories and biographical info kept on subjects for reference, now retrieved electronically

- Editorial Conference—every day the top editors meet to discuss positioning and coverage.
- Copy desk—where the copy editors check spelling, style, grammar, and fact, and where pages are laid out and heads are written.

Technology

- Letterpress—printing off a raised surface—first change occurred in the 1950s.
- Offset—a photoelectric transfer—more economical, faster, looks better.
- Significant Trend in Weeklies and Small Dailies—centralized offset printing.
- OCR (Optical Character Readers)—uses a scanning device.
- VDT (Video Display Terminal)—more sophisticated—keyboard connected to CRT.
- All newspapers today use some form of computerized cold-type setting.
- Today the reporter not only gathers and writes, but also edits and typesets.
- Pagination—positioning and layout electronically
- Plateless printing—the printed word will be applied to rolls of newsprint by computer-controlled ink jet technology

Characteristics of Newspapers

Metropolitan Dailies—150,000 plus

1. **Reader Identification**—Inevitably, the gap between reporter and reader is much larger than with smaller papers.
2. **Specialization**—A major hallmark of the met press is specialization—for everyone from the elevator operator to the third assistant managing editor. Reporters and editors may specialize in politics, education, medicine, science, and even human interest.
   a. The key figure in this type of paper is the city editor, who may have as many as 100 reporters under him. Most of these reporters are given specific assignments.
3. **Speed**—The big city paper may publish as many as five or six editions a day. So rigid are the deadlines that a precise minute-by-minute flow of copy or photographs is maintained through each department right up until press time.
4. **Sunday Editions**—As traditional in American homes as the Sunday afternoon dinner is the Sunday morning family newspapers.
   a. feature stories, interpretive pieces, and elaborate photographic layouts
   b. enormous amounts of retail and institutional advertising
   c. specialized sections covering everything

The Weekly Newspaper

1. The weekly is characterized by its intimacy. Everyone knows the editor and the reporters who work on the paper.

2. The weekly is the core of community life—it is the chief source of information about the activities of individuals and organizations. It serves as a unifying force in the community.

3. The staff is generally small and a few people perform a variety of tasks. The work is long and hard because there are so few to do it—gathering news, editing it, selling advertising, handling circulation, and overseeing the printing.

4. A typical staff would be about six persons.

5. There is no wire service and every story and picture is of local origin—the paper depends on stories from housewives, club secretaries, etc.

6. The range of editorial excellence among weekly papers is wide.

7. Most publish on Thursday because it is a day when local merchants want to reach readers with news of their weekend sales.

8. The development of offset printing and computer typesetting has greatly helped the weekly papers in that they were the first to take advantage of it, not having large sums tied up in capital equipment.

9. Most weeklies are produced today by offset, either in their own plants if the paper is large enough to justify the investment, or in a central plant along with several other weeklies.

10. Weeklies are rarely the crusading type with some outstanding exceptions. Most editors see their role as that of printing constructive, orthodox news without dealing in sensationalism. There is some division as to editorials. Most feel that editorials and opinion columns give personality to the newspaper and leadership to the communities. Others fear alienating readers and advertisers. The papers often stimulate thinking, particularly on local problems and projects.

11. Many have shifted from subscription by mail to newsboy delivery and some have turned to free distribution to attract more advertisers.

12. Weekly chains covering several neighboring communities from a central editorial and printing plant are increasing.

The Field Today

1. Weekly newspaper readership, unlike that of U.S. dailies, is increasing substantially—up 30.3% since 1980 to a 1991 total of 63.5 million with advertising revenues improving.

2. Many community papers (about one-third), especially suburban weeklies, have in recent years decided to give their papers to every household in the circulation area to please large advertisers.

3. The papers face strong competition from shoppers—free newspapers containing primarily advertising.

4. Nearly every community weekly and daily is a member of its state press association, which confers the political and commercial benefits of size on a large group of small papers. This helps in legislative representation, advertising representations, awards, and the sharing of information.

Career Opportunities

- Freedom and flexibility—a wide variety of areas to cover.
- A closeness to the audience.
- Opportunities for growth—knowledge of advertising, production, circulation, etc.
- The community environment—quality of life.
- A chance for ownership.

Technology: The Desktop Revolution

1. Desktop publishing equipment has enabled small operators to save money on typesetting and provide readers with more imaginative typefaces and design features.
2. The typical system involves:
   a. A personal computer with at least 512 kilobytes of memory.
   b. A laser printer.
   c. Computer software including word processing graphics and page-layout programs.

Small Dailies (below 25,000 cir.; typically between 7,500 and 15,000)

1. The greatest difference between the small daily and weekly is timeliness.
2. Generally, geography determines why some towns have weeklies and others have dailies. When a big town is close by, competition from the big neighboring daily may make successful operation of a small daily impossible.
3. Reporters and ad sales reps are not necessarily better—but they must be faster. A small daily has proven to be an excellent training ground for all journalists. It gives a reporter the opportunity to cover more areas and do it every day.
4. As circulation increases, so does the staff.
5. Costs are much greater and advertising is essential. Most papers try to average better than a 50-50 ratio and some will go as high as 65% advertising.
6. The small daily, like the weekly, publishes all the local community news possible, but also relies on the wire services and feature syndicates to fill the space.
7. New technology has greatly helped this paper also.
8. The home delivery subscription list is the backbone of a successful circulation system. The carrier buys the papers for several cents cheaper than they are sold to subscribers for.

Medium-Sized Dailies (25,000 to 150,000 cir.)

1. Papers of this size are financially strong enough to have editorial staffs of considerable scope, usually with persons of outstanding ability. It is excellent training for reporters aspiring to bigger and better things.

2. This papers exists in (1) communities the size of Lubbock that are located long distances from metro areas and (2) in the suburbs where the papers, and the advertisers, have gone where the people with buying power live.

3. Suburban papers have a median staff size of about 100, including 26 editorial employees.

4. The staff titles may resemble those on the metropolitan dailies, with duties expanded.

5. This size paper publishes a big Sunday edition and serves many small communities nearby.

6. It provides the reader with detailed local community news along with almost as much press association and featured material as the metropolitan dailies do.

7. The home delivery carrier again is the backbone of this type of paper.

8. Only in the larger cities with heavy commuter traffic on public transportation do street sales have the importance they once did.

Minority and Ethnic Press

1. Despite affirmative action legislation and court decisions striking down barriers of racial discrimination, we continue to see underrepresentation of minorities in newspapers. Approximately 12.07 of daily newspaper journalists are minorities. Minorities represent about 25% of the population of the country.

2. A survey conducted by the national Association of Black Journalists indicates that African American journalists feel that they work in an unfriendly, unsupportive environment.

African American Press

1. The first Black newspaper was *Freedom's Journal* in 1827, started by John Russworm and Samuel Cornish. "We wish to plead our own cause. Too long have others spoken for us," they said.

2. Close to 50 Black publications followed *Freedom's Journal* before the end of slavery. There have been a total of 5,539 to this date.

3. Today there are 400 Black newspapers. Only 11, however, had founding dates before 1900. The average life span has been nine years. Buying power is $85 billion.

Hispanic Press

1. Hispanics and Latinos make up the fast growing segment of the U.S. population. There are 35 million Hispanics—12.5% of total population. There will be 50 million by 2060. 53% say they pay more attention to Spanish media and 43% show loyalty to those who advertise in Spanish media. Buying power is $350 billion.

2. The Hispanic press can trace its roots to the area that is now Texas in the 1810s.

3. Today there are 550 Hispanic dailies and weeklies.

Native American Press

1. The history of the Native American Press is undocumented.

2. Today about 280 reservation newspapers serve Native Americans. This is also like a return to authoritarianism because of the rigid controls placed on these papers by tribal councils.

Asian Americans

1. The fastest growing minority in the country. Underrepresented in media fields.

2. Ownership consists of 25 newspapers and 12 radio and TV stations.

In General

Readers, journalists and advertisers have abandoned minority newspapers in favor of white-owned newspapers.

1. Publishers complain that as middle-class readers abandon the inner cities for the suburbs, they drop their subscriptions along the way.

2. Many college-educated minority journalists prefer the potentially higher salaries and broader opportunities available at white-owned media.

3. Ad agencies, always sensitive to demographics, remain hesitant to place ads in minority newspapers.

4. Also, competition from minority-owned media, such as radio and magazines, has hurt newspapers.

Convergence

1. Most newspapers are now delivering news online.

2. Most provide their news and information for free.

3. The battle on the Web centers on classified advertising.

4. Newspapers must do more than simply put their printed news online. Many newspapers are hiring individuals to generate news for their Web pages.

5. We are now seeing people trained in both print and broadcasting as part of their preparation to deliver news in this new age.

6 Magazines

Role of Magazines

1. The magazine exists to inform, entertain, and influence its readers editorially and to put before them ad messages of national or regional commercial organizations.

2. The magazine writer probes the "why" of a situation and is an interpreter of events far more than a newspaperman can be.

3. A newspaper cannot be aimed at a single special interest group and survive. Yet hundreds of successful magazines are designed for reading by such limited-interest groups as gas station operators, dentists, etc.

Background/Development

1. Andrew Bradford reportedly beat Ben Franklin in issuing the first magazine, the *American Magazine,* in 1741.

2. By 1830 there were more than 300 magazines; most of them represented literary, abolitionist, temperance, or other movements.

3. As railroads linked the country together in the 1840s and 1850s, magazines, for the first time, had a chance to cultivate national audiences and sell national advertising.

4. Cheap bulk rates established by Congress also helped.

5. Magazines began to appeal to the masses in the 1880s and 1890s.

6. We have already discussed the muckraking movement of the early 1900s.

7. As magazines began to grow, some of the big names included: *The New Yorker, Time, Reader's Digest, The Saturday Evening Post, Life, McCall's, Good Housekeeping,* and the *Ladies' Home Journal.*

8. TV put a serious dent in advertising revenue for magazines beginning in the 1960s.

9. Magazines lowered their prices to compete and spent money on promotional efforts. Overhead costs produced red ink.

10. In the 1960s the *Saturday Evening Post, Collier's, Life,* and *Look* all died.

11. Their death created the false impression that hard times had hit the big magazine field.

12. This was not the case. Individual magazines have suffered because of: (a) changing public tastes and marketing conditions, (b) increased postal rates, and (c) loss of advertising to TV.

13. As the bigger general magazines faded, they were replaced by smaller and more specialized magazines.

Magazine Leaders

Largest Circulations

1. *Reader's Digest:* 9.3 million U.S. circulation monthly plus 12 million in 60 foreign countries; founded 1922 by DeWitt Wallace.

2. *TV Guide:* 9 million circulation weekly (regional editions), founded 1953 by Walter Annenberg, runs articles as well as logs.

3. *Modern Maturity:* 24.4 million monthly. A membership publication of AARP.

Photojournalism Emphasis

1. *National Geographic:* 5 million circulation monthly, third largest of U.S. magazines; founded in 1888 by National Geographic Society; became photojournalism leader in 1970s with eclipse of *Life* and *Look.*

2. *Smithsonian:* 1.7 million circulation monthly, founded 1970 by the Smithsonian Society.

3. *Ebony:* 1.3 million circulation monthly; founded 1945 by John H. Johnson in Chicago as a black version of *Life;* became leading black magazine for middle class with mostly home circulation.

News and Opinion Magazines

1. *Time:* 4.1 million weekly circulation; founded 1923 by Henry Luce and cornerstone of Time, Inc. (*Fortune, Life, People, Sports Illustrated, Money*); leading U.S. news magazine.

2. *Newsweek:* 3.4 million weekly circulation; founded 1933, currently owned by Katherine Graham of the Washington Post; successful rival to *Time* and preferred by some for its division of news and opinion (runs columnists).

3. *U.S. News and World Report:* 2.3 million weekly circulation; founded in 1948 by David Lawrence in merger of earlier publications; based in Washington and contains a mixture of news and opinion.

4. *National Review:* 110,000 weekly circulation, founded in 1955 by William F. Buckley, Jr.; strong, intelligent voice of the far right in American politics; independent-minded in party affairs.

5. *New Republic:* 75 to 80,000 weekly circulation; founded in 1914 by Herbert Croly and Walter Lippmann as voice of literate liberalism.

Business Magazines

1. *Fortune:* 650,000 circulation, founded in 1930 by Henry Luce; edited for businessmen, strong photographic and design qualities.

2. *Business Week:* 760,000 weekly circulation; founded 1929 by the McGraw-Hill Publishing Company; reviews economic trends, business and industry news; one of 30 McGraw-Hill publications.

Literary Quality

1. *Harper's:* 300,000 circulation monthly; founded in 1850, owned since 1965 by John Cowles, Jr., Minneapolis newspaper publisher; traditional literary emphasis new secondary to public affairs.

2. *Atlantic:* 337,000 circulation monthly, founded in 1857; has retained more of its literary flavor than *Harper's.*

3. *Saturday Review:* 530,000 weekly circulation; founded in 1924; expanded from literary interests to cover the arts, travel, current affairs.

4. *New Yorker:* 632,000 circulation weekly, founded in 1925 by famed editor Harold Ross; known for distinctive writing, cartoons, public affairs reporting. Recently, Tina Brown, former editor of *Vanity Fair,* has taken over as editor and has made major changes.

5. *New York:* near 400,000 circulation weekly, founded in 1968; aimed at youthful city dwellers; bought in 1977 by Rupert Murdoch, Australian publisher; now more a city magazine.

6. *Esquire:* 835,000 circulation; founded in 1933 as a monthly magazine for men, now every two weeks; famed for publishing fiction of leading U.S. writers, New Journalists.

Women's Interest

■ Primarily designed for women, they have increasingly aimed content at both sexes. They no longer contain stilted love stories and flattering stories about society matrons. They include *McCalls* (5.1 million), *Ladies Home Journal* (5 million), *Good Housekeeping* (4.7 million), *Family Circle* (4 million), *Woman's Day* (3.9 million), and *Better Homes and Gardens* (7.6 million).

■ A second category is the movie and TV magazines.

■ A third concentrates on special categories or age groups such as *Harper's Bazaar, Seventeen, Ms.* and *Sportswoman* reflect the women's movement.

■ Supermarket publications such as *Family Circle* (4.6 million.) are also popular. *National Enquirer* (3.7 mil.) is aimed at women as well.

Men's Interest

- Sports, adventure and sex dominate magazines in this category.

- Leaders in sports are *Sports Illustrated* (3.4 million.) (swimsuit edition 41 million), *Sports Afield,* and *Field and Stream.*

- Tops in adventure magazines are *True* and *Argosy.*

- A phenomenon of the 1960s has been *Playboy* (3.4 million), which replaced *Esquire.*

- A number of handyman magazines, such as *Popular Mechanics* and *Popular Science,* have always had large circulations.

Religious or Denominational Publications (1,300)

Other Publications

- Geography—international, country, state, local
- Gender
- Ethnic
- Age
- Lifestyle
- Occupation
- Hobby
- Socioeconomic Background
- Application
- Ideology

SUNDAY SUPPLEMENTS

Among magazines with the largest circulations are those distributed with most Sunday newspapers. The leaders are *Parade* (36.1 million), *Family Weekly* (12 million) and the black publication *Tuesday* (2.4 million).

COMPANY PUBLICATIONS

Traditionally known as house organs, these are put out by industrial and business firms to their employees, salesmen, dealers, and stockholders.

With a circulation above 300 million, American business and industry invest more than $600 million a year in these publications, which are either (1) internal or (2) external.

Desktop Publishing

This new phenomenon has enabled editors and publishers in recent years to produce, at relatively low cost, thousands of special magazines and newsletters, as well as numerous other publications.

With only a personal computer, software, hard-disc drive and a basic laser printer, one operator can write, edit, set type, prepare artwork and lay out an entire publication, which is camera-ready to go to a printer.

Marketing Magazines

1. Magazine revenue comes from circulation and advertising, built upon strong editorial content.

2. At one time publishers sold each copy to the reader for far less money than it cost to produce it, making their profit through the sale of advertising.

3. Now, subscriptions and single sale prices account for 52% of total revenues as compared with 48% for advertising. Advertising revenue has risen in 10 years from $6.7 billion to $17.7 billion.

4. Successful publishers must convince advertisers that the purchase of space in their pages is a good investment. This proof is based mostly on circulation figures.

5. Achieving a balance between newsstand sales and subscriptions is also an important consideration. What is on the cover is used to market or sell the magazine on the newsstand.

Format Changes

1. Magazines must show either very large mass distribution figures among a general readership, or a firmly established circulation among the special interest groups to which their publications appeal editorially.

2. Editors of big magazines have had to make major changes in content to counteract the element of fictional entertainment brought to their readers by TV.

3. Many new magazines are started each year. Some find a market and are successful—some don't and fail. Between 250 and 350 new magazines are announced each year and the odds are 10 to 1 that a new magazine will fail.

General Magazines

General magazines appeal to advertisers for two reasons: (1) their nationwide distribution carries a commercial message from coast to coast and often overseas; (2) their use of quality-paper stock presents a colorful, attractive, and realistic-looking ad.

Specialized Magazines

1. The specialized magazines offer advertisers a unique advantage—a selective audience for selective products.

2. The small magazines offer lower advertising rates than the general ones, an obvious advantage for the advertiser trying to reach a specific group.

3. To counteract this, the large magazines are now offering advertising space on regional or fractional split-run bases.

4. Many of the large magazines are now printed and distributed regionally. Plates are prepared at a central plant and then flow to presses in several parts of the

country. Therefore, identical copies can be run and delivered on the same day from coast to coast.

5. Most magazines do not own their own printing plants. Large, privately owned job printing companies print most of the national magazines.

Editorial Content and Operation

1. Editorial content is predominantly nonfiction. About 75% of material in consumer periodicals is factual and the percentage is even higher in trade and professional journals.

2. Most editorial staffs are relatively small—especially those that draw on the work of "freelance" writers. The typical setup includes:
   a. Editor-in-chief—editorial direction, content and cover
   b. Managing editor—coordinating editorial, art and production
   c. Department editors
      ■ Senior editor—heads up major feature department—supervises writers, designers, and photographers.
      ■ Associate editor—second-level editor
      ■ Staff writer/reporter—researches, writes and edits material in assigned subject areas.
   d. Photography editor
   e. Art/Design editor

3. The editor's job is to decide what kind of material he wants to publish, arrange to obtain it, and then present it in such a way as to be pleasing to his readers.

4. Most editors work from a formula—each issue contains specified types of material in predetermined amounts.

5. The editor has assistants to screen free-lance material, work with writers, think of ideas, and edit material chosen for publication.

6. He will have an art director to arrange attractive layouts and select the cover.

7. The use of a photojournalist is playing a bigger role in most magazines today.

8. A key part of most magazines' operations is the editorial conference in which the editors discuss the forthcoming issue, and make decisions on the material to be used. Each magazine is planned months in advance of publication.

9. The news magazines operate differently. They must employ larger staffs and maintain bureaus throughout the country—even internationally.

10. Most magazines have at their command large amounts of freelance material—most of the unsolicited material never is used.

11. Most general magazines go out and commission the better writers to prepare material for them. This is a good arrangement because they don't have to worry about paying a full salary with benefits.

12. Some of the better freelance writers use agents to sell their output.

13. With luck and perseverance freelance writers can sell material to smaller magazines and even hit the big mags with anecdotes, personal experience, humor,

and photography. The process starts by sending a query letter—briefly what the writer has in mind.

14. Big mags will pay $5,000 and up per article. They pay from .75 to $1.50 a word. If you write a 5,000-word article, you could earn $5,000. You would have to write 10 articles and have them all accepted to earn $50,000 before expenses and taxes.

15. Since 350 to 300 individuals make a living as freelance writers, it would be well for one to freelance as a hobby or a sidelight. It is also a good idea to study the magazine you want to sell to, and tailor your article to fit that magazine and its special interest group.

16. There are probably three groupings of freelance writers. The first are those who are proven and highly sought after—very few in number. The second would be those who have had some success but have not reached the top level—a large number. The third would be those trying to get established—a very large number.

17. This requires great perseverance.

18. The best approach is to use a query letter, in which you outline what you are proposing to write.

UNIT II: STUDY GUIDE

1. Identify the following individuals: Thomas Jefferson, Alexander Hamilton, Benjamin Day, James Gordon Bennett, Horace Greeley, Joseph Pulitzer, William Randolph Hearst, Henry Luce, Adolph Ochs.

2. Identify the following items or periods: The New England Courant, the colonial press, "Common Sense," the Penny Press, the personal press, the New Journalism of the 1880s, Yellow Journalism muckraking, *The New York Times*, tabloids, New Deal journalism, World War II, Korea and Vietnam, the New Journalism of the 1960s, advocacy journalism, "In Cold Blood."

3. What does a newspaper have to do to be considered outstanding?

4. What is the newspaper's role in current society.

5. Describe the role of a reporter.

6. Why did circulation decline in the late '60s and '70s? What did publishers do to attract more readers?

7. Describe the impact of *USA Today*.

8. Describe the impact of computers in the newspaper business. Identify the following: hot type printing, offset printing, OCR, VDT, pagination.

9. Describe the characteristics of (1) the weekly newspaper, (2) the small daily, (3) the large daily, and (4) the metropolitan daily.

10. What is the role of magazines today?

11. Describe the following magazines: largest circulation, photojournalism, news, quality or class, women's interest, men's interest, business, company.

12. Where does the revenue come from that enables a magazine publisher to make a profit?

13. Discuss the general magazine's appeal vs. the appeal of the specialized magazine.

14. Describe how a typical general circulation magazine is organized.

15. Identify Helen G. Brown and Hugh Hefner.

16. What dies the magazine writer do that the newspaper editor can't do?

- Describe early newspaper editors.

  Not editors, printers

- Describe early newspapers. What problems did the New England Courant have?

  Not Newspaper

  political Propaganda

- What contributions did Franklin make?

  Made Journalism Respectebl

- What role did Hamilton and Jefferson play?

  used papers to support their POV

- What role did Thomas Paine play?

  Motivational essays

- Where did the term "Penny Press" come from?

  Newspapers in 1830s dropped to a penny

- Who was Benjamin Day? James Gordon Bennett? *— known for news gathering*

  First to PennyPress

- What contribution did Horace Greely make?

  gave editorial page an indpedent voice

- What does the term "personal editor" mean?

  Personality of editor avershown the newspaper itself

- How and when did the first press association start?

  1848 in NY two corespondents covered the Mexican war

- Who was Joseph Pulitzer?

  Symbolized the modern approach to Journolism

- What was "Yellow Journalism"?

  the circulation wars between Pulitzer and Hurst

- What was "Muckraking"?

  magazine movement on corruption in US.

- Describe the tabloids of the 1920s.

  wildly sensational

- Who was Henry Luce and what did he contribute?

  Started time magazine, 1923

- What was the nature of journalism in the New Deal period?

  Brought about specialization

- What was the New Journalism of the 1960s? (three parts)

  1. writing of New nonfiction 2. advocacy writing/taking sides 3. investigative reporting

- Which war was the first TV war?

  Vietnam

- What is considered to be our greatest newspaper?

  New York Times

- What must a newspaper do to be considered outstanding?

  comprehensive coverage   great writing/reporting   progressive leadership

- What are the primary functions of a newspaper?

  To inform, interpret, serve

- What has been the pattern on newspapers since 1900 in terms of numbers and circulation? What has caused changes?

  # of papers has gone down   circulation has gone up

- What did studies in the 1960s show about declining readership?

  identified young people and low income minorities as not reading papers

- What was done to change this situation?

  made cosmetic and coverage changes

- Are there more morning or afternoon papers?

  morning by far

- What are current circulation figures doing in relation to population growth?

  Newspaper circulation is declining

- Why is the family owned newspaper becoming a thing of the past?

  They are selling them to avoid inheritance taxes

- Define a group.

  two or more

- What percentage of dailies are controlled by groups?

  two-thirds

- What is intermedia competition?

  TV. competition

- Is it better to have one financially strong newspaper in one city than two weaker ones?

  One strong than two week

- What has encouraged many independent newspapers to sell to groups?

  tax lawes

- What percentage of reporters are Black and Hispanic?

  12.07%

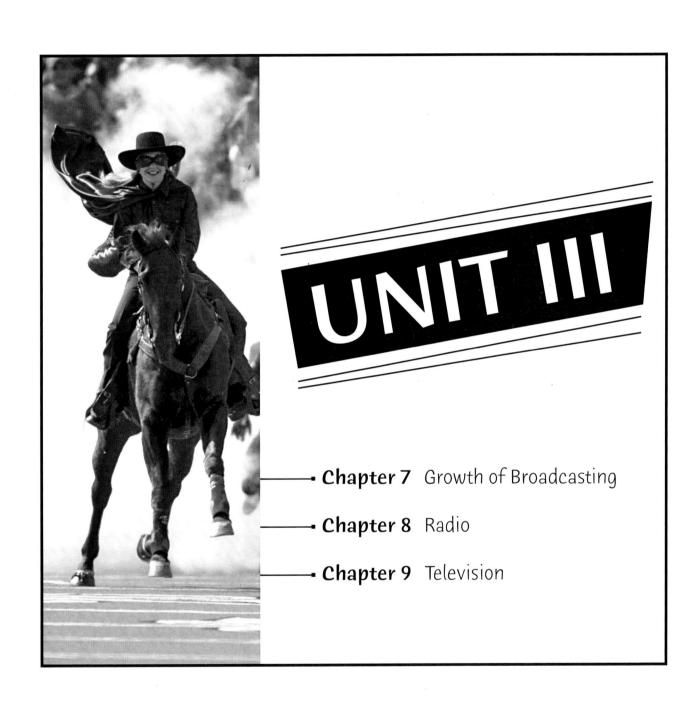

UNIT III

Chapter 7 Growth of Broadcasting

Chapter 8 Radio

Chapter 9 Television

7 Growth of Broadcasting

Early Broadcasting

1. Dr. Lee DeForest, the father of radio, made the first news broadcast on November 7, 1916. He reported the returns from the Wilson-Hughes presidential election.
2. World War I radio greatly restricted private broadcasting.
3. David Sarnoff, another radio pioneer, began advocating radio as a household utility in the same sense as the piano or phonograph.
4. He became a principal in the Radio Corporation of American when it was formed in 1919.
5. Dr. Frank Conrad, a Westinghouse engineer in Pittsburgh, broadcast music in 1919 and stimulated the sale of crystal sets.
6. Westinghouse-owned KDKA became the country's first fully licensed commercial station on November 2, 1920, although the *Detroit News* had started WWJ as an experimental news station on August 31, 1920.

Early Development of Stations

1. Newspapers helped start many stations as a kind of novelty. They thought it would be a good way to tease listeners and get them to purchase newspapers.
2. Companies like GE, Westinghouse, and RCA also helped to start stations so they could sell the receiving sets.

A Profit Incentive

1. In 1924, the Eveready Battery Company began to sponsor programs on radio stations as an experiment. It stimulated the sale of their batteries.
2. Now there was a profit incentive to start a radio station and many stations now began to develop.

Development of Networks

1. With more stations on the air there was a need to provide program material for those stations—hence the development of networks.
2. AT&T organized a chain of 27 outlets soon afterward from WEAF to Kansas City.
3. RCA, Westinghouse, and GE formed another chain—mostly along the East coast.
4. AT&T retired from network ownership in 1926 in an agreement by which it obtained control of the electronic relay system.
5. RCA, Westinghouse, and GE then formed the NBC network in 1927; the old AT&T chain was called NBC Red and the other NBC Blue.
6. In 1930, Westinghouse and GE withdrew, leaving RCA the sole owner of the NBC networks.
7. Also in 1927, the Columbia Phonograph Record Company helped organize what became the Columbia Broadcasting System under William Paley.
8. In 1934, WGN in Chicago and WOR in New York formed a third network, the Mutual Broadcasting System.
9. In 1943, faced with pressure by the FCC, NBC sold its Blue Network to a group that formed the American Broadcasting System in 1946.

Legislation

1. As mentioned in the first unit, the Radio Act of 1927 created the Federal Radio Commission to govern the number of stations in an effort to avoid mass interference. The commission also authorized 50 powerful "clear channel" outlets to provide remote areas with programming.
2. In 1934, the Communications Act renamed the regulatory agency the Federal Communications Commission.

Radio Entertainment

1. Like TV today, radio was considered an entertainment medium in the 1930s.
2. Most of the formats you see on TV today started on radio with one major exception—radio played on the imagination.
3. The programs included situation comedies, comedy variety shows, soap operas, westerns, dramas, quiz shows, adventure programs, children's programs, and musical shows, to name a few.
4. Three ingredients were essential: scene setting, the use of sound effects, and the play on the listener's imagination.
5. In the early days, scripts were read before live audiences. There was no tape to edit out mistakes.

Some Sidelights on Old-Time Radio

1. *The Shadow:* The Shadow had the ability to cloud men's minds, making him invisible so he could go about solving crimes and aiding the police. The opening proclaimed, "Who knows what evil lurks in the hearts of men's minds? The Shadow knows!" During the war with Germany, listeners wrote the network demanding to know why Lamont Cranston was not using his secret powers against the Nazis.

2. *Fibber McGee and Molly:* In every episode Fibber would begin to look for something he had misplaced and would say, "I know, I left it in the hall closet." Molly would then say, "Don't open that door, McGee!," but he would open it, and out would pour a pile of junk, courtesy of the sound-effects people. This caused millions of Americans to use the line "Fibber McGee's closet," thinking of a closet in their own homes crammed with junk.

3. One of the most popular shows was a comedy about two Black men, played by two white men, Amos and Andy. So popular was this program that movie houses promised to stop the film and turn on the radio so their audiences could listen to the show.

4. Americans took to radio in the depression-ridden 1930s and the audiences began to grow. It became an American pastime to listen to the radio.

5. Proof positive of radio's ability to play on the imagination was the famous "War of the Worlds" Broadcast directed by Orson Welles on the CBS Mercury Theater of the Air on October 30, 1938.

   You must remember the state of the world in 1938. Germany was invading its European neighbors and Americans felt they would be drawn into the war. October 30 is also the eve of Halloween.

   The story was about an invasion of Earth by Martians in giant machines, landing in Grover's Mill, New Jersey. The script, adapted from the H.G. Wells story, was constructed as if a normal evening of broadcasting was being interrupted by bulletins about the invasion, and so forth. The story began with the normal disclaimer, but apparently listeners paid no attention and actually believed that we were being invaded.

   Immediately after the show began at 8:00 P.M. on Halloween night, the police began calling CBS studios, asking them what was going on. The police and newspapers were besieged with calls from people reporting that they had seen Martians in their neighborhoods.

   Highways along the East Coast were jammed with motorists. A power failure in a small town in Washington was all that was needed to convince residents there that the end was indeed upon them.

   The program scared the hell out of millions of Americans. Oddly enough, it was only being broadcast on one network, but it was a huge demonstration of the power to radio to play on our imaginations. Finally order was restored, but the FCC insisted on some changes designed to prevent other occurrences of this nature. You can imagine how many listeners the program had the following week. You can also imagine the interest that advertisers now had in the program.

Newspaper-Radio War

1. In the Depression of the 1930s radio grew and prospered because it was free. Advertisers began to shift advertising to network radio and away from newspapers.

2. This angered the American Newspaper Association, and they forced the press associations to stop selling news to radio.

3. A compromise, the Press-Radio Bureau, began in 1934. Press associations would sell the networks news if the networks would stop collecting their own. The networks would be furnished with two five-minute newscasts daily and bulletins. It failed.

4. The networks then began to recruit journalists to gather their own news.

Radio News Comes of Age

1. In the late 1930s, radio news abruptly came of age. In 1938, Americans listened intently for news from Europe. The Munich Crisis was one of many such events. Americans got up very early each morning to listen to the rantings of Hitler. Radio was personal—it came right into your home with live coverage.

2. As a result, radio news became very popular and broadcasters like Edward R. Murrow, CBS's news chief in Europe, became household personalities.

3. Murrow's broadcasts from London during the German bombing were classic. He had a journalistic background and a great radio voice.

4. Radio was the first to report the attack on Pearl Harbor and President Roosevelt's declaration of war the next day.

5. Radio was able to bring listeners major news stories first, although the transmission was not always great and the details were sketchy. Newspapers still provided the details.

6. Radio brought listeners news of the D-Day invasion, the dropping of the Atomic Bomb, and the signings that ended the war in Europe and in the Pacific.

Postwar Expansion

1. The five years after the war ended were high water-marks for radio. The number of stations doubled and listeners now embraced both the entertainment and the news formats.

2. By 1950, there were 2,086 AM radio stations on the air and 80,000,000 receiving sets.

3. Frequency Modulation (FM) Broadcasting picked up, but did not catch on like it would later.

4. In 1948 CBS, in anticipation of the coming of TV, staged a talent raid on NBC and signed such stars as Amos 'n Andy, Burns and Allen, Edgar Bergen, and Bing Crosby.

Enter Television

The development of television, halted during World War II, moved quickly in the late 1940s. The breakthrough year was 1948. Networks were shifting their attention to television as were sponsors, cognizant even then of popularity ratings.

1. Experimental Television Broadcasting—in the United States it began in the 1920s.
2. There were some stations offering regular schedule in the late 1930s.
3. The wartime freeze left only six pioneer stations on the air.
4. After the war there were 41 stations on the air in 23 cities.
5. Live TV signals had to be transmitted by means of a coaxial cable. This was expensive and time-consuming. Live programming was restricted to a small area of the East coast.
6. In 1948 the FCC imposed a freeze on all existing TV applications in order to work out an orderly plan for the development of television.
7. The Freeze ended in 1952—and the FCC announced its plan:
   a. To assign more than 2,000 channels to nearly 1,300 communities.
   b. To extend telecasting—from the Very High Frequency channels (VHF), 2 through 13, to 70 more Ultra High Frequency channels (UHF), numbered 14 through 83. (Television-set manufacturers were not required to include both UHF and VHF tuning until 1964.)
   c. To reserve 242 channels for educational television stations.
8. The transcontinental microwave relay was completed in 1951, which replaced the coaxial cable and greatly speeded up the transmission of live TV programming.
9. With the end of the freeze many more stations began to appear. NBC and CBS were ready to go into TV. ABC was not ready and would occupy a distant third place for years to come. There was an ill-faded Dumont TV Network, which only lasted a few years. CBS, as a result of the talent raid in 1948, took a leading position and would hold it until the 1970s.
10. In 1955 there were 439 stations and 33 million receivers; by 1965 there were 588 stations (90 UHF), 114 educational outlets, and 61 million receivers, or 93% of U.S. homes.

Television Entertainment

1. Milton Berle was TV's first great star, going on the air for NBC in 1948 with the Texaco Star Theater.
2. Many programs, both network and local, were inferior by today's standards, but audiences didn't care—it was new and different and you could see it.
3. In many markets TV programs were delayed several weeks because the microwave relay system took time to spread. Programs were shipped in cans to affiliate stations.

The 1950s

- Ed Sullivan's variety show
- Lucille Ball and *I Love Lucy*
- *The Today Show* began in the early 1950s.
- *Davy Crockett* debuted in 1954 on the *Disney Wonderful World of Color* program.
- In 1958, Lucy was displaced in the number one spot by *Gunsmoke*—then came a flurry of Westerns—*Wagon Train, Bonanza,* and others.
- *Star Trek* began in the mid 1960s.
- Detective shows also became popular in the late 1950s and early 1960s with considerable violence—resulting in a public outcry.
- Perry Mason began in 1957, followed by the *Twilight Zone* in 1959.
- The big quiz show scandal revolving around the *$64,000 Question* broke in 1959.

The 1960s

- One of the big hits in the early 1960s was the *Dick Van Dyke Show* (featuring Dick Van Dyke and Mary Tyler Moore), 1962
- Johnny Carson took over the *Tonight Show* in 1962. *A Charlie Brown Christmas* debuted in 1965.
- In the late 1960s, the top shows were the *Smothers Brothers Comedy Hour* and *Laugh-In.* Also rated high were situation comedies like *Gomer Pyle, The Beverly Hillbillies,* and the *Andy Griffith Show. Dean Martin's Show* also was popular. *The Fugitive* debuted in 1967.

The 1970s

- The 1970s saw the demise of the westerns and the rise of programs that dealt with touchy issues like *All in the Family* and *Maude.* Shows featuring minorities became popular—*Chico and the Man, Sanford and Son. The Waltons* was a favorite, along with *M.A.S.H.,* bringing back memories of the Korean War.
- *The Mary Tyler Moore Show* was a spin-off of the earlier *Dick Van Dyke Show* and it produced a spin-off of its own, as did the *Carol Burnett Show.*
- CBS led the pack in introducing soap opera-type shows into prime time.
- ABC finally came to the front after 25 years of being last with shows like *Happy Days, LaVerne and Shirley,* and its 1977 smash, *Roots.*
- Controversial shows like *Three's Company* and *Soap* also were popular.
- Throughout it all, there were always big audiences for performers like Bob Hope, Lucille Ball, Perry Como, and a regular, *Walt Disney's Wonderful World of Color.*

FROM "THE MAN WHO DESTROYED TELEVISION" BY GARY DEEB IN *PLAYBOY*

To paraphrase Howard Beale, the anchorman in the movie *Network,* the people are mad as hell—and they're not gonna take it anymore.

That's the reason behind the coming viewer revolution. The people hate television—even though most of them are irresistibly attracted to it. As inarticulate as this rage may be, it's significant for what it stands for: The people are striking back at the networks that have trampled them and treated them like slobs for so long.

Since 1977 viewing levels have dropped for the first time in history—anywhere from two to eight percent. The falloff is even steeper for the audience of the three major networks. The Washington Post recently revealed that a survey showed that 53 percent of people 18 and older are watching less TV than five years ago.

Silverman, the subject of the article, moved from WGN in Chicago to CBS in 1962, where he soon invaded the Saturday-morning children's block with loud, violent cartoons featuring jet-age super heroes. Later he became chief of the CBS weekday soap operas and game shows.

In 1975 he went to ABC as chief programmer. That autumn, he took a long hard look at our country and made a fateful discovery: He recognized that millions of lazy, incompetent parents would gladly surrender the TV to their kids all night—that an increasing number of people seemed to be abdicating any sense of parental responsibility.

Under Silverman, in three short years, was created a subculture of boorish heroes and fantasy figures who became the favorites of youngsters everywhere—from the braless wonders on *Charlie's Angels* to the classroom morons on *Welcome Back, Kotter.*

Tits 'n zits. ABC quickly became the "Sweathog network."

Silverman created: *Three's Company, Charlie's Angels, Happy Days, Laverne and Shirley, Soap, Starsky and Hutch, Vegas, Welcome Back, Kotter, The Ropers, What's Happening, Donny and Marie, Carter Country, Operation Petticoat, The Love Boat, Fantasy Island, Hardy Boys Mysteries* and *Battles Star Galactica.*

CBS and NBC frantically trying to make up lost ground, carbon copied and TV sank even lower. It was like monkey see-monkey do.

The network honchos began to program against one another, itching their most popular programs from night to night attempting to knock off the heavily publicized premiere of a rival program. The American viewer cannot be sure what's on any of the three networks on a given night.

Silverman also developed a promo marketing campaign that elevated the promo to an exalted position. CBS and NBC followed suit.

Silverman moved to NBC in 1978 and found himself fighting himself—this time unsuccessfully. He resigned this summer.

Nielsen places its audiometers in "typical" U.S. households—that is, homes in which the family watches a ton of TV. Network insiders insist that if a Nielsen household registers relatively light viewing for a few months, the black box is placed in one where TV viewing was epidemic.

Therefore, TV networks enjoy artificially high audience ratings.

The 1980s

- NBC, after being pushed to the bottom, made a comeback in the 1980s.

- In 1981 the network had dropped to a pre-tax profit mark of $48 as compared with $152 million in 1977.

- Grant Tinker replaced Silverman. He placed faith in the right people and let them do their jobs. He stuck with low-rated, high-caliber shows such as *Cheers, St. Elsewhere,* and *Hill Street Blues.* Patience paid off.

- His first prime-time schedule was 1982–83, which boasted a freshman class of *Cheers, Family Ties, Remington Steele, St. Elsewhere,* and the mid-season replacement hit, *The A-Team.*

- He then scored with *Miami Vice, Highway to Heaven, the Golden Girls,* and *The Cosby Show.*

- In 1986–1987, NBC led the ratings. They have been a consistent winner ever since.

- Network profits began to rise, reaching a record $333 million in 1985.

- Fox, initiated by Rupert Murdoch in 1987, has gone from Sunday night only to five nights in 1990. He had big hits with *The Simpsons* in 1990–91 and *Beverly Hills 90210* in 1991–92.

The 1990s

- In 1992, CBS finally got back into the No. 1, thanks in part to its coverage of the Olympic Games, and NBC dropped to second.

- Many of NBC's new shows did not work. The network played it safe and left aging shows on the air too long. It had dropped to third place after a No. 2 in the 1991–92 season. They had to try to attract young audiences.

- NBC decided to cancel two popular shows, *Matlock* and *In the Heat of the Night,* because ratings showed that they appealed to a 50+ audience and the advertisers want to reach younger audiences.

- NBC also lost *The Golden Girls* and *The Cosby Show* at the end of the '92 season.

IMPACT OF FOX

1. Fox's biggest consistent show was *The Simpsons.*
2. *Beverly Hills 90210* was a big hit.
3. Fox has also added other look-alikes, but the only one that lasted was *Melrose Place.*
4. The *X-Files* became a Sunday night fixture.
5. Fox then shocked the TV world by outbidding CBS for NFL football, which caused ripples and turnovers in many markets.
6. They then added NHL hockey.
7. NBC began a comeback in the mid-90s with *Home Improvement, Seinfield,* and *ER.*

The 2000s

- In 2000–01 new reality shows, like *Survivor* and *Temptation Island,* were hits.
- *The West Wing* had a banner year on NBC.
- *Law and Order* nabbed its largest audience in its 11-year history.
- *Friends* was a big hit for NBC.
- NBC took back the lead in 2002.
- The decline of *Who Wants to Be a Millionaire* hurt ABC.
- *CSI* was the top new show on any network. (CBS).
- *American Idol* has been a blockbuster for Fox.

Television News

1. TV news, like radio news, was slow to develop. Network news started out in a 15-minute format, as did most local news programs. These early newscasts were crude—radio news on TV.

2. Edward R. Murrow put his radio show "Hear It Now" on TV as "See It Now" in the early 1950s. In a 1954 program, Murrow took on Senator Joseph McCarthy and exposed him as a demagogue.

3. As TV began to cover major events producers began to discover that there was a big league type audience for news.

4. Highlights:
   a. McCarthy-Army hearings
   b. Kefauver crime subcommittee
   c. U.N. sessions
   d. 85 million saw the great debates of the 1960s between Nixon and Kennedy
   e. Kennedy opened his news conferences to live TV in 1961
   f. Cuban missile crisis
   g. 135 million saw some part of John Glenn's 1962 first manned orbital flight
   h. Upwards to 80% of the U.S. saw coverage of the Kennedy assassination and the subsequent shooting of Lee Oswald (NBC live)
   j. 93% saw the Kennedy funeral
   k. Neil Armstrong's walk on the moon, July '69

5. The three networks gradually began to increase their budgets for news.

6. Walter Cronkite emerged as the top news personality on CBS.

7. NBC used two anchors, Chet Huntley and David Brinkley.

8. ABC has struggled with its news approach—Howard K. Smith, Peter Jennings, Harry Reasoner and Barbara Walters (which bombed), but has made great strides recently with new faces like Ted Koppel.

9. The cable networks, CNN, MSNBC, and Fox, have changed the landscape for national TV news. No longer do viewers have to depend on CBS, NBC, and ABC for their source of news. This has lessened the power of the networks and the anchors who work for them. For many years Dan Rather (CBS), Peter Jennings (ABC,) and Tom Brokaw (NBC) dominated the national news scene. Rather was ousted by CBS, Brokaw retired, and Jennings died of lung cancer. Their replacements have not been able to command the audiences of the past.

Radio's New Format

1. In the late 1940s popularity shifted from audio to video, which spelled financial losses for the radio networks. Local radio stations continued to do well because they served community advertisers who could not always afford the costs of TV.

2. TV, for all practical purposes, killed network radio as it had developed in the 1930s, 1940s, and 1950s. Many predicted that all of radio would die.

3. But radio stations adopted a new format—music, news and sports, centered around a personality known as the disc jockey.

4. The networks continued to broadcast news, sports, and special events, but gradually all the old radio entertainment programs went off the air.

5. The number of stations increased from slightly over 2,000 in 1950 to over 4,000 in 1965. FM experienced a spurt of popularity with the new music formats.

6. Stations then began specializing in certain types of music—adult listening, popular music, which changed from rock and roll to the rock music of today, and country-western. Some stations have all-news formats.

8 Radio

Overview

1. We have already traced the development of broadcasting through (1) the "Golden Days of Radio," (2) the coming of age of radio as a news-gathering and reporting medium, (3) the changes brought by the coming of television, (4) the development of television, and (5) the influence of the FCC.

2. It should be pointed out initially that broadcasting is basically different from the print media in that:
   a. It is controlled by an agency of the Federal Government
   b. It does not exist primarily to present news and related material—it exists as an entertainment medium
   c. Most broadcast stations, unlike newspapers, are highly competitive with other stations for viewers

The FCC

Composed of 7 commissioners appointed by the President and confirmed by the Senate. It began operating in July, 1934 and is divided into four bureaus. The most important is the Broadcast Bureau, which authorizes and regulates all broadcast services. It allocates space for radio and TV use, assigns frequencies, grants licenses (7 years), and reviews the station's performance.

FCC Decisions

1. **The Fairness Doctrine**—we have already discussed this and its impact. In August, 1987, the FCC voted to eliminate this rule. The members said it was unnecessary because of the large number of radio and TV stations serving the country, and was unconstitutional because it gives the government editorial control over broadcasters. This does not change the "personal attack rule," which makes stations

offer individuals a "reasonable opportunity to respond" to personal attacks or the "political editorial rule," which requires stations to offer response time to station editorials.

2. **Limits on Ownership**—In 1964 the FCC limited ownership to no more than 7 AM, 7 FM, and 7 TV stations (5 VHF and 2 UHF). In the summer of 1984 this was changed to 12-12-12 and has now been changed to 30-30-30. In 1971 the FCC ruled that no station owner could now acquire another station in the same community.

3. **Prime Time Rule**—In the late 1960s the FCC limited network prime-time (7–11 EST) programming to three hours. This was done to encourage locally produced programs. It has not worked very well.

4. **Counter-Advertising**—proposed by the FTC to the FCC, it would force radio and TV stations to offer time—free time—to anyone who wanted to challenge the contents of a commercial under the Fairness Doctrine concept. This has been a hotly debated topic and was not acted upon by the FCC.

5. For many years the FCC forced radio and TV stations to the following:

    a. community ascertainment requirements—hearings and surveys to ascertain community issues. The stations were then required to demonstrate how their programming had addressed these issues.

    b. commercial requirements—no more than 18 to 20 minutes of advertising in an hour.

    c. non-entertainment programming—(radio) devote 8% of AM programming and 6% of FM to news, public affairs, etc.

    On April 3, 1981, the FCC dropped all three requirements to allow broadcasters to "follow their own path in determining how to serve their communities' needs." In addition, detailed programming records are no longer required.

Growth of Radio

1. Despite all that is said about TV's growth and economic impact on society, radio continues to draw a "big-league" audience.

2. Through trial and error it has developed a new personality following the crisis that arose when TV emerged in the 1950s. The "Top 40" station emerged which played music and news and attracted loyal audiences.

3. Despite the impact of TV, the number of radio stations has grown steadily over the years. TV killed network radio, but not radio.

4. About 96% of all Americans 12 and older listen to radio as opposed to about 66% who watch TV in a day.

5. Over $25 billion a year is spent on radio advertising.

6. During the past 12 years FM radio has grown tremendously to the point where it controls 75% of the radio audience.

Talk Radio

1. Nowhere is contemporary radio more alive than in the call-in talk shows, both local and national. Talk radio became a "hot" item in the 1990s. It includes everything from advice on personal relationships to politics.

2. Foremost among the talk shows hosts is Rush Limbaugh, whose program is carried by over 600 stations.

3. Satellites have made it possible for radio talk shows to go national. Most programs have someone who screens all calls.

4. Others who have big audiences are Larry King, Dr. Laura, Bill O'Reilly, Shawn Hannity, and Howard Stern, whose shock-talk approach offends some but is liked by others.

5. 22% of all Americans over 18 listen to talk radio on a regular basis.

Formats

1. Whatever your taste in music, you can find it on a radio station.

2. FM stations have been able to better shape their programs for specific age ranges and listening preference.

Music Programming

1. The key figure in music programming is the disc jockey—a personality.

2. Stations usually play the top forty songs in the particular format that they feature.

Radio and the Recording Industry

1. Radio depends on the recording companies for the flow of new songs to keep its shows fresh—the industry also needs radio to play its music.

2. The recording industry is highly promotional and emotional in nature, subject to quick switches in the public mood.

3. In the 1950s and 1960s, radio went through the payola scandal where disc jockeys took cash or gifts to favor certain records on the air. This continues to some extent today.

4. Following the scandals in the 1950s and 1960s, DJs were stripped of their authority to pick records. Instead, station managers hired program directors or music directors to make selections. Another route used was to hire outside consulting firms to prepare the play list.

5. Recordings have also become the most potent mass medium of protest and anti-establishment on the American scene—sometimes challenging traditional values.

6. Lyrics of contemporary records frequently allude to drugs and sex, at time in terms so frank that broadcasting them to a general audience may be questioned.

7. Co-called "rap" music has created considerable unrest among adults and parents, especially when the music seems to advocate violence against law enforcement officials.

8. Stations may refuse to air certain selections.

9. Some disc jockeys also have gone beyond conventional boundaries of good taste in emphasizing their points and demonstrating their right of free speech.

10. The U.S. Supreme Court has ruled that broadcasters do not have a constitutional right to air obscene words that apply to sex and excretion.

News Coverage

1. Radio's programming flexibility enables news bulletins to go on the air immediately. This is one big advantage it has over TV in news.

2. In the days when all stations were required to do news, the quality suffered because many stations did not have the ability to make the financial investments necessary to have a good news department.

3. In those days we had the "rip-and-read" approach. Disc jockeys would run into the wire room and rip off the latest news summaries, then go back and attempt to deliver them on the air as news, without any preparation.

4. Many stations just took stories from the local newspaper and rewrote them to be read over the air. Some don't even bother to rewrite.

5. There are still wide differences between the types of news broadcasts, but deregulation has allowed stations who do not have the ability to develop a news department to just concentrate on playing music. Stations that want to do news generally do a decent job of it. The process has improved because of deregulation.

6. News staffs are expensive to maintain, so it is understandable that so many small stations cannot offer much quality, and constantly turn over news directors and newscasters.

7. Over the years sports is the one constant on radio as coverage of high school, collegiate, and professional sports is still a staple.

Public Radio

1. Throughout its history public radio has had to scramble for funds.

2. A series of budget cuts in the current climate has represented a huge problem for National Public Radio.

3. NPR programming is frequently provocative; powerful critics, both inside and outside Congress, accused it of reporting news and public affairs in a biased manner.

The Economics of Radio

1. Radio stations have only one thing to sell—time.

2. A station charges for commercials based on the size of its audience.

3. Commercials are run in between recorded music, and this has influenced the record companies to limit songs to about three minutes.

4. Radio sales reps stress demographics—income, education, occupation, ethnic background, marital status and buying behavior. Most stations have a target audience based on the type of programming they present.

5. Radio, like TV, depends on surveys and polls. Arbitron uses a diary method to conduct local ratings. The biggest advantage that radio offers to advertisers compared to TV is lower cost, both for airtime and for preparation of commercials. Radio is also more flexible. It does, of course, lack visual appeal. Radio ad sales reps claim that you can, in fact, see radio commercials thanks to good scripts, creativity, sound effects, and the play on the imagination.

6. Frequency is a key to success in radio advertising.

Current Trends

1. New engineering advances should continue to enhance radio's portability, convenience, and sound fidelity.

2. Multimedia packaging, special events and promotions, and partnerships with retailers are proving to be effective marketing strategies.

3. Satellite transmission can cut costs by 50% or more and often delivers better sound quality complete with well-produced music shows, highly professional disc jockeys, and network quality news. This becomes an appealing package to advertisers.

Internet Radio

- Between 1996 and 2001 the number of stations programming over the Internet increased to 5,000. In 2001, the Internet radio industry began to backtrack because of concerns over unauthorized use of advertising online.

- The boom became a bust

Satellite Radio

- XM began broadcasting in late 2000 and Sirius came on board the next year. They have now merged.

- Satellite radio comes free for the first six months in many vehicles.

- It has become increasingly popular.

No other medium can reach as many people throughout the world, and reach them as quickly, as radio.

9 Television

The Impact of TV

1. Television has the ability to take an obscure performer and project that person into a national celebrity—almost overnight.

2. It helped make possible the election of a bright young senator named John Kennedy.

3. In news and special events, TV has the ability to project the viewer into the activity more powerfully than any other medium.

4. It helped end the war in Vietnam by bringing the death and suffering into our living rooms every night.

5. It also showed a lack of a national resolve that encouraged our enemies in Southeast Asia and actually prolonged the Vietnam War.

6. It brought about more rapid changes in civil rights than might have been the case.

7. Critics say it has also made "passive blobs" of many children and has eroded our interest and skill in reading.

8. Critics contend that certain personality types cannot handle the violence so ingrained in many TV programs. More than one brutal crime is directly attributable to an idea present during a TV prime time drama. The four major networks have agreed to begin providing a warning to families.

9. It has encouraged terrorists in the Middle East who hijack airliners and kidnap Westerners.

10. It has the ability to dictate when events will be staged so as to obtain coverage. Good examples can be found in the scheduling of news conferences and sporting events (football games that begin at noon, the World Series played at night.)

11. TV has always had its share of critics. In 196l, the then chairman of the FCC, Newton Minow, labeled much of television programming "a vast wasteland." That feeling continues today.

12. TV yields large profits because advertisers have found that commercials on TV sell merchandise in such enormous quantities that they will pay very high prices for airtime to broadcast those commercials.

13. The cost of a typical 30-second network TV commercial depends upon its rating. The higher rated shows obviously charge more. The Super Bowl charges in excess of $3 million for a 30-second commercial. Its audience normally runs between 120 million and 130 million.

14. All TV stations were required to broadcast exclusively in digital beginning June 12, 2009 (originally February 17, 2009). About 11% of homes were not ready for the transition. There are 1,655 stations in 210 U.S. markets that were delivering a digital TV signal in advance of this deadline.

Decline of the Networks

1. Network viewing in the 1980s and 1990s has been hurt by:
   a. Cable TV and satellite TV
   b. A growing number of independent stations
   c. Home video, including Internet-delivered video

2. In 1978 the three networks drew 93% of the audience. Today it has fallen to 41%.

3. As a result, NBC, CBS, Fox, and ABC have made substantial investments in the cable business.

4. They have also gone head-to-head with the Hollywood studios and production companies that make most of the entertainment programs seen on the networks. The networks had been restrained since 1980 from producing more than five hours of network shows. That expired in 1990 and, in 1993, the FCC gave the networks the right to produce as much of their prime-time shows as they want, own stakes in shows produced by outsiders, and syndicate reruns of their shows abroad and enter the U.S. syndication market by 1995.

5. In the past, these independent production firms produced the shows and sold air rights to networks.

6. The network supervised the stories used and has the final word on casting. Its censors approved the scripts. Ownership of the shows, however, remained with the production firm. TV networks and syndicators now battle for syndication dollars.

Structure of Television

1. Just as in the newspaper business there are many small stations, a large range of medium-sized stations, and those that operate in huge metropolitan areas. Staffing relates to those sizes.

2. The typical station would be headed by a general manager who supervises the major departments: chief engineer, program director, news director, sales manager, business and promotion. A typical size staff would be about 100 people, depending on market size.

3. Of the approximately l8 to 24 hours a day the station is on the air it only creates about 3 or 4 hours of its own programming, mostly local news.

4. Sources of income:
   a. The network, which pays an affiliate based on the size of the station's market. This is why there is concern of declining network audiences.
   b. National spot commercials the station puts on the air during station breaks.
   c. Local and regional commercials.

5. An affiliate contracts with a network for the exclusive right to broadcast in its coverage area all programs distributed by the network. It also has the right to refuse to broadcast any network program.

6. To supplement network and local programming a station will purchase syndicated shows for a flat, negotiated fee. All commercial time slots are then open for local advertising.

7. An exception to this arrangement has been a syndicated show where the station does not pay for the show, but only gets about 50% of the break time for its own commercials.

8. Another variation used by the networks is to provide an affiliate with a show without the normal compensation but leaving enough local spots to enable the station to make a good profit. NFL football is a good example of this arrangement.

The Battle for Viewers

1. We have already discussed some of the strategy involved when the networks wage a battle for viewers personified in the ratings.

2. CBS was a consistent winner for years until Fred Silverman came along at ABC and made great gains in the late 1970s with a number of youth-oriented comedies, more sexual and contemporary in tone than the other networks.

3. NBC, after dropping to third, hired Silverman, then fired him, and was led out of the wilderness by Grant Tinker to a number one ranking in 1987. This lasted until the late 1990s and early 2000s, when networks like CBS and Fox began programming reality shows such as *Survivor* and *American Idol*. These shows allowed these networks to overtake NBC in the ratings at different times.

4. Networks begin a major fanfare for each new show during the summer—along with their returning shows.

5. The odds against any specific program being placed on a network are very high.

6. The hours at which a program is shown, and the nature of the programs the rival networks put on the air against it, may be the deciding factor in its survival. This sometimes produces a nightmarish combination of variables.

7. In the past, network program executives moved programs from time slot to time slot. A new show may follow an established hit or be programmed between two hits. A top-rated show may be placed against a rival network's news show to send it under. This is not in the best interests of the viewers.

8. Of course, public tastes constantly change.

9. The networks are constantly looking for good "spin-off" possibilities—taking a popular character from one situation show and building a new series of programs around that character.

10. Executives know the kind of programming that sells. None of them care to do much daring experimentation, and the result is predictable formula programming in prime time. This has a ripple effect throughout TV because much airtime on independent stations is filled with these network reruns. This was demonstrated by the rash of reality shows beginning in the early 2000s.

11. The network does not have total control over the affiliate unless it owns the affiliate.

12. The typical affiliate may opt not to show something very controversial. It may carry a local sports team in place of a network show.

13. The networks spend a great deal of time trying to create enthusiasm among the affiliates for their shows.

The Ratings

1. The ratings are used to sell advertising. They are not unlike circulation figures used by newspapers.

2. The A. C. Nielsen Company does the network ratings. They select a sample of 5,000 homes—that represent the viewing habits of between 99 and 110 million American households. Therefore, they create a sample audience and measure the viewing habits of that audience. From this data they estimate the number of viewers in the entire population watching a program.

3. Nielsen uses a measuring device called a people meter. This device is a small hand-held instrument with 8 numbered buttons, each for a family member. Users feed their sex and age info into the people meter. They are supposed to punch in when they begin watching and punch out when they leave the room.

4. Nielsen has a computer-dialed telephone call from the Nielsen center in Florida to each of the homes in the sample automatically collecting data twice a day.

5. Nielsen supplements people meters with audits and quality checks. In the past they have used diaries placed in 2,400 homes and each week one-quarter (600) are asked to submit a detailed outline of the week's viewing.

6. Telephone interviews and personal interviews are also used to supplement the electronic and diary information.

7. Local ratings use the diary method. Local TV stations, outside huge metropolitan areas, are rated four times a year. This is called the sweep months—November, February, May, and July.

8. These reports give back two kinds of data:
   a. Market: The group of people reached by a given TV station.
   b. The program rating—the number of sets tuned to a particular show in relation to the 110 million TV households in America. A program with a rating of 20 was watched by persons in 22 million homes; the program was seen in 20% of all homes equipped with TV in the nation.

c. The audience share—the percentage of sets in use while the particular program rated was broadcast. Assume that at 9 P.M. on Sunday night there are 110 million households and 100 million are watching TV. If 30 million households are watching a show on Fox, its rating is calculated by dividing 110 million into 30 million (viewers/total population WITH television) for a rating of 27 and a share of 30 because you divide 30 million into 100 million (viewers/total population actually with a TV set ON).

9. Today, information called people data is becoming more important to advertisers as opposed to home data. Advertisers want to know who is watching. In the late 1950s and the 1960s the best audience for advertisers was men and women, 19–35—they are more gullible and absorb ad messages more readily.

10. This is called demographics. It is one reason why CBS canceled *Red Skelton, Ed Sullivan, Mayberry RFD,* and *The Beverly Hillbillies*—they appealed to older people in rural areas, neither of whom are considered good buyers.

11. Today, women 19–49 are now considered to be the best buy.

12. The critics maintain that ratings merely indicate what is the most popular of what is offered, but not true preference. People probably really don't know what they want because they are unaware of the vast possibilities. Whenever you attempt to please everyone, you usually wind up pleasing no one.

13. There is also criticism that to be a Nielsen viewer a person must regularly watch TV and that many groups are slighted—minorities especially make this complaint.

14. The ratings are not inherently evil themselves. It is how the medium uses them. Broadcasters do not select programming on the basis of its merit and then use the rating system to count heads, so that they would know how much to charge the advertiser. Instead, they program to build audiences so they can charge high ad rates.

Sex and Violence—Are the Media Weakening Public Morality?

Violence on TV, a national concern for decades, escalated into the 1990s as the networks, cable, and individual stations competed for audiences and revenue. Today, 37% of all programming on American cable and network TV featured themes high in violence.

The effects of viewing acts of violence on TV by the public, especially children, has been debated for years.

Effects of TV Violence

■ The effects of viewing acts of violence on TV by the public, especially children, have been debated for years. In 1972 the Scientific Committee on TV and Social Behavior spent $1 million in a two-year study to determine whether or not there is a cause-effect relationship

■ In 1972, the Scientific Committee on TV and Social Behavior spent $1 million in a two-year study to determine whether or not there is a cause-effect relationship between TV programs that depict violence and aggressive behavior in certain subgroups. They found that social scientists could not agree that there was a cause-effect relationship with the exception of (1) those who were unbalanced and (2) children.

■ TV violence can cause aggressive behavior and aggression, concluded an American psychological Association task force in 1992. The average child witnesses 8,000 murders and 200,000 acts of violence on TV by the time he or she reaches age 18.

■ Public concern over televised violence has intensified with news reports that a young woman was fatally set on fire with kerosene in a Boston neighborhood soon after a similar scene had been depicted on TV.

■ A suit was filed against NBC over a TV movie, Born Innocent, which depicted the rape of a 15-year-old girl with a plumbing device in a mental hospital. This act was re-enacted on a 9-year-old girl with a bottle in San Francisco. The attackers admitted they had seen the movie.

■ In Milwaukee a 39-year-old man who wanted to "scare" his wife was being held Tuesday on suspicion of setting fire to her shortly after he watched a TV movie about a woman who burned her abusive husband to death.

■ In Florida a 15-year-old was given life for murdering his 83-year-old neighbor. His parents sued all three networks, claiming that TV programming showed the impressionable teenager how to kill.

■ This suit, and others, have been dismissed on First Amendment grounds.

■ Interviews and studies abound regarding this subject, with considerable agreement by psychologists and sociologists that watching violence on TV and at the movies indeed makes some children more violent.

■ In the mid-70s the networks began to insist that senseless mayhem on Saturday cartoon shows and acts of violence in general be toned down.

■ In the fall of 1975 the networks responded to FCC and Congressional pressure and began devoting the first hours of prime time viewing to programs suitable for family viewing—and were promptly sued by the Writers Guild for "prior censorship," inhibiting the creative artists' efforts to depict the world "as we know it."

■ An advisory system has also been devised to warn parents that a program might be unsuitable for viewing by children.

■ Despite all this, the annual "violence profiles" for all network programming showed that, after a decline in 1977, the level of violence on all three networks is rising. Researchers recorded 1,846 acts of violence during a single day of broadcasting.

■ Complaints continued to be lodged by numerous groups, including the PTA and the so-called Moral Majority.

■ Stations, of course, may also view controversial programs and do not have to air them.

■ News departments have also begun to develop guidelines on how to report demonstrations and riots, but have refused to give any ground in the coverage of violent news.

■ The arguments continue today with the conclusions basically being unchanged.

Tabloid TV

1. The news-information-tabloid magazine program has gained increased popularity . . . *A Current Affair, Inside Edition, Hard Copy.*

2. These programs have pushed mainstream TV and newspapers to offer more details about sex, violence, and other subjects that once were treated gingerly.

News

1. There are three basic differences between broadcast journalism and print.
   a. The broadcaster excels in "actuality" reporting.
   b. The broadcaster prepares his report to be heard.

   GUIDELINES FOR BROADCAST NEWS WRITING
   - Write less formally than for print
   - Round off figures
   - Qualify sentences at the beginning
   - Avoid attempts at clever phrases
   - Be careful not to panic your listener
   - Avoid long lists of names
   - Avoid strange and awkward sounding words and phrases
   - Keep stories brief

   c. Broadcasting relates the latest news, seldom details.

2. Because of the impact of on-the-scene reports and the believability of those anchoring the news, annual surveys have found that a large percentage of the public regard TV news as more believable than newspapers. Television also has the following advantages:
   a. its ability to tell stories visually from the scene of the action making viewers feel as though they are at the scene themselves.
   b. the ease with which viewers can receive the news.
   c. the fact that TV news is delivered by attractive men and women whose personalities create an aura of intimacy.

3. Rivalry among the networks is intense, especially in the early evening newscasts.

4. For many years, three anchors—Tom Brokaw (NBC), Peter Jennings (ABC), and Dan Rather (CBS) dominated TV news. Then Brokaw retired, CBS retired Rather, and Jennings died.

5. The three network newscasts were basically all the national news Americans received until the 24/7 cable networks began in the 1990s. This has drastically impacted the three networks. It has diluted their power to dominate the news agenda of viewers.

6. It has also lessened the influence of the anchors.

7. All three networks supplement their daily newscasts with detailed background on occasional big stories through special half-hour programs—sometimes an

hour. ABC's *Nightline,* now a regular late evening newscast, was born in the Iranian captive situation. These are newsmagazines that began to receive high ratings in the late 1990s.

The most notable success in public affairs programming outside the regular news is CBS' *60 Minutes,* which earned $70 million in profit in 1985. It also became the highest-ranked show in the weekly Nielsen ratings in the 1984–1985 season. Other networks have followed suit: ABC's *20/20* and *Prime Time Live,* and NBC's *Dateline.*

NBC is the number one network in terms of profits compared to ABC and CBS. Its news division (including NBC News, MSNBC, and MSNBC.com) had pre-tax profit of $400 million in 2008. However, the economy is forcing news divisions for all three networks to cut costs by cutting staff.

8. Interview Shows: *Meet the Press* and *Face the Nation* are weekend shows where journalists interview one or more prominent people in the news.

9. Morning News Shows: *The Today Show* (NBC in 1952), *Good Morning America* (ABC), and CBS compete for viewers each morning with a variety of news, interviews, personality profiles, weather, etc. as does CNN and Fox.

10. Local TV news is also a big item. It is the one way in which a local station creates an "image" with its viewers. Most programs are 30 minutes long and appear at noon, 6, and 10. However, the most news reporting is usually less than 23 minutes.

11. In TV words must be correlated with film—what the newscaster is saying and what the viewer is seeing. There is a preoccupation with pictures.

12. The development of high-speed film was a major breakthrough. The perfection of videotape was another. In the typical TV setup today there is a considerable amount of "electronic newsgathering equipment."

13. Local news is rarely able to escape the clutches of show business considerations.

14. Many stations use consultants, called "news doctors," to establish news and programming policies. These people are not journalists.

15. The personality of a TV newsperson is critical. On camera people may hold or lose their jobs on the basis of measured physiological response by sample audiences. (Christine Craft and KMBC-TV in Kansas City) (Connie Chung)

The Quality of Interviewing

1. Too many reporters seem to want to put words in a subject's mouth.

2. In small to medium markets, stations often employ people with little experience and the quality of interviewing suffers as a result. This is not a criticism. They have to learn somewhere. It is a fact of life.

Public Television

1. Public TV attacks about one-seventh of the median weekly viewing accorded to commercial TV.

2. It is funded from (1) government grants, (2) underwriting grants from large corporations, and (3) contributions.

3. In 1966 the Carnegie Commission on Educational TV recommended the formation of a public TV system.

4. Congress, in 1967, established the Corporation for Public Broadcasting, which created PBS, replacing the old NET network in existence at the time.

5. There have been some very successful programs—*Sesame Street and The Electric Company, Masterpiece Theater, Ken Burns's The Civil War* and *Baseball,* and a variety of public affairs type programs. *The Lehrer News Show* is another example.

6. But despite many successes, critics have attacked the network as programming for a well-educated elite minority.

7. Conservatives and moderates have attacked the network as having become the "Welfare of the Airwaves" for liberal and left-wing elites.

8. Pressures to balance the budget and the Reagan administration's negative attitude toward funding have had a negative impact on funding through Congress.

9. PBS was severely tested in 1980 when the Mobil Corporation, one of its major underwriters, publicly questioned its decision to show the British program, "The Death of a Princess." The film dealt with the public executions of a Saudi Arabian princess and her commoner lover, for adultery. The Saudi Arabian government expelled the British ambassador and put pressure on Mobil, which had a heavy interest in Saudi oil. The program aired, and only 7 stations did not carry it.

10. Viewers perceive many valuable assets in public television but their allegiance does not run deep.

Cable TV

1. Cable TV was first introduced after World War II to improve TV reception in the valleys of eastern Pennsylvania and the mountains of Oregon. Initially, then cable systems served small, remote communities by picking up programs from distant stations and piping them by cable into a subscriber's home.

2. In the late 1950s cable television served 550,000 subscribers through 560 systems. By 1969 there were 3.6 million subscribers and 2,260 systems. By 1977 the numbers were 12.5 million and 3,800 systems serving 17.3% of the nation's homes.

3. In 1981, there were 18.3 million homes being served by 1,212 companies.

4. There are **7,832** cable systems in the country and there are **65.2 million** cable homes. Another **40 million** households have digital cable, **39 million** have Internet access via a cable modem, and **19.6 million** have telephone service from the cable company.

5. We have already discussed the negative impact cable has had on networks.

6. The cable boom began in 1975 when the Sitcom satellite was successfully placed in orbit. Time, Inc. leased space on a communication satellite to distribute HBO to participating cable system operators. Then Ted Turner leased space to beam the signal of WTBS to a satellite then back to cable systems around the country. This was followed by WGN in Chicago and several others.

7. There have been a number of interesting developments in the cable business since it started.
   a. Local governments award cable franchises.
   b. The FCC attempted to regulate cable initially. They saddled cable with numerous rules and regulations. The cable industry often went to court and the Supreme Court voided some of the most onerous federal regulations. Finally, in 1980, the FCC symbolically tossed in the towel and junked their rules.
   c. In 1984 the Cable Communications Policy Act eliminated the control local governments once had over fees charged subscribers. As a result:
      - Cable system operators immediately raised their prices. In 2007 the basic cable average cost was $42.76.
      - Large corporations purchased scores of cable systems.
      - Cable system operators became investors in the networks that produce the programs their systems showed.

   In 1992 Congress passed a law over President Bush's veto giving the FCC authority to regulate basic cable rates. All local over-the-air television signals in their coverage areas must be included in the basic cable package.

8. In 1985 the U.S. Court of Appeals in Washington voided the FCC's must-carry rule at the request of the broadcasters. It offered local stations the alternative of negotiating with their cable system a license fee that the cable system would pay for carrying a local station's programs.

9. In 1992 the FCC permitted the Big Three national networks to own cable TV systems.

10. Approximately 75% of the cable firms are owned by individuals and companies that have other media interests as well.

11. Companies have poured millions into lively bidding for monopoly urban franchises in places like Dallas and Houston. Since franchises are awarded by city councils, there have been numerous squabbles and lawsuits.

12. It is also very expensive to lay cable in large cities, and cable companies do not want to lay cable in low-income areas.

13. Advertising is accepted by most of the cable systems. Advertising revenues for cable was $26 billion in 2008.

Premium or Pay TV

- Pay TV has been around since the 1950s.

- In 1977, following the launch of Home Box Office, the Supreme Court overturned an FCC regulation placing limits on movies and sports events that could be shown on cable TV. The Court refused to review a U.S. Court of Appeals decision that pay cable TV would not adversely affect either public interest or over-the-air TV, and that the FCC had no authority to regulate pay TV (*FCC v. Home Box Office*).

- Earlier, as mentioned, in 1975 HBO began sending signals to a satellite and back to earth. Initially it served about 8,500 viewers. It now serves close to 20 million homes.

- At least **20 million** also take a pay service.

- Offerings range from family entertainment movies to R-rated adult films to soft-core films. There are 11 in all.

In General

1. In 1996 Congress passed a new phone and cable law. It did the following:
    a. Permitted local and long-distance telephone companies and cable operators to enter each other's business.
    b. Loosened limits on how many TV or radio stations a firm or individual can own.
    c. Banned obscene material on computer services and the Internet computer network. (overturned by the SC)
    d. Required manufactures to include a computer chip in new TVs that would recognize shows labeled as violent. Parents could block shows they don't want kids to see.
2. Competition from Direct Broadcast Satellite: There are **28 million** DBS satellite homes.

Video

1. Enthusiasm began to grow for VCRs when TV fans discovered the advantage of taping their favorite programs when they were gone and preserving programs in a video library. In 2007, DVDs overtook VCRs—now 81% of all homeowners in the U.S. own a DVD player.
2. Innovative entrepreneurs then began to obtain the rights to a few motion pictures and then offer them for rent or purchase.
3. Video shops blossomed in every city. Supermarkets and department stores installed video departments.
4. The Supreme Court ruled in 1984 that Americans are legally entitled to videotape shows and movies from TV for personal use.
5. In 1986 filmmakers began to issue movies with great depth and a high level of performance aimed at the over-30 age audience sitting at home. On average, Americans rent 2 DVDs per month. In 2007, DVD rental was a $7.5 billion business.
6. Sex-oriented movies, the outright X-rated ones as well as softer R-rated ones, became big attractions in video.
7. Hundreds of long-forgotten movies have been returned to life to satisfy VCR owners hungry for movies to view. Adventure series, situation comedies, and collections of music videos that had disappeared from the TV screen were resurrected and distributed as videocassettes.
8. Today there are 51,000 video titles on the market, enough to fill 18 months of around-the-clock viewing.
9. Combined rental and sales income of VCRs in the retail market in 1989 were estimated at $11.5 billion a year.
10. Theater owners have been angered by the early release of first-run movies.

11. Other roles of videos:
    a. Videos taken by individuals and turned over to news broadcasters.
    b. Self-help and how-to tapes.
    c. Training tapes for corporations, trade associations, etc.
    d. Children's programs.
    e. Education.
    f. Politics.
       ■ Recruit volunteer campaign workers.
       ■ Present the candidate in the most favorable light possible.
       ■ Raise money.

12. Advertisers are wanting to insert commercials into videos and more ads are now appearing in videotapes.

13. Cable TV is fighting the video surge with pay-per-view and "On Demand" TV where the family can pay to see a popular new movie before the video is released. This can be ordered by phone.

14. Where does all this lead?
    a. Will excessive watching of electronic material in private isolate viewers from normal participation in the affairs of society?
    b. Will dependence on packaged electronic visual material for entertainment and instruction deprive children and adults alike of the desire to read?
    c. In the future, will we have to pay for things we have viewed for free?

- Describe radio of the 1930s, 1940s and 1950s. What did its format resemble? What techniques did it use? *Same format as today sound effects and imagination*

- Was private broadcasting permitted prior to 1920? *KDKA*

- What was the first fully licensed radio station? *KDKA*

- How much attention did early radio stations pay to news? *Not much*

- Why did newspapers start many of the early radio stations? *They thought it was a fad and tried to use it for advertising*

- What caused the growth of network radio? *advertising*

- What was the first major radio network? What year was it formed? *NBC 1947*

- Why was the Federal Radio Commission formed? Under what philosophical argument? *To give guidance to stations*

- What happened to radio during the Depression? What was the Press Radio Bureau? What did networks do when the wire services cut off news? *It prospered since it was free something that failed they hired their own people to gather news*

- Who was Edward R. Murrow? *covered the European War WWII and became a household name on the radio*

- What happened to radio in the post-World War II days? *It grew and prospered*

- Why was live TV programming restricted in the 1940s? *Co-axial cables*

- What promoted the growth of nationwide TV? *Satellite/microwave relay system*

- What two problems has TV entertainment always suffered from? *1. underestimating audience intelligence 2. over exposure*

- Who was the undisputed leader of TV shows in the early 1950s?

  Lucille Ball

- What CBS program ushered in a new era in prime time entertainment?

  All in the Family

- Who was Fred Silverman?

  chief programmer for ABC and took them to #1

- What happened to radio when TV became a nationwide medium?

  it changed to music

- Describe the first network newscasts.

  crude / radio news on TV

- Describe the impact of TV on John F. Kennedy.

  First TV president

- When did TV news turn the corner?

  when JFK was assassinated

- What are the three differences between broadcasting and print media?

  Broadcasting is regulated print isn't

- Can the FCC censor?

  No

- What were the FCC policies on community ascertainment, commercials, and non-news programming? What finally happened to these requirements? What about license renewal—how long?

  No more than 18 minutes of commercials
  It was all dropped   *Started at 3 years now 7*

- What is the prime time rule?

  4 hours in the evening

- Compare radio listening to TV viewing today.

  43%

- What are the differences between AM and FM radio?

  FM had stereophonic sound

- What type of audience listens to radio?

  Specialized audience

- What is the relationship between radio stations and recording studios?

  They are interdependent

- Describe radio news. Why do some stations not do news?

  It's flexible they can't afford it

- Are all individuals who deliver news on the air considered journalists?

  No some are presenters

- Describe the power of TV.
  Power to dictate times of events

- How much profit does a typical TV station make?
  23 - 24% pr

- How much is a 30-second commercial on the Super Bowl?
  2.4 mil

- What is an affiliation agreement in TV?
  you agree to carry network programing

- Who has been the producer of most network shows?
  independent production programing

- What are the odds for success of new programs on TV?
  Not good

- Who rates national TV programs? How is this done?
  Nelson company   The put people meters in t,000 homes

- What is a major criticism of ratings? What do broadcasters do with the information they get from ratings? Do ratings determine the life and death of TV shows?
  Demographics not represented
  Yes

- What is the No. 1 demographic buy in TV today? What was it 15 years ago and why?
  women A-49
  It was 19-29

- Why is TV news important to local TV stations?
  It gives their personality

- What are the three differences between TV news and print news?
  1. actuality reporting
  2. Prepare things to be seen
  3. gives you the latest info not all details

- What is one of the major problems in local TV news?
  show b.z

- In broadcasting where do you often give your source?
  At the beginning of the sentence

- What is the impact of public broadcasting?
  Not much

- How is public broadcasting funded?
  tax dollars private gifts grants

- How was PBS created?
  By congress through

- Does the FCC control cable?
  No

- The growth of cable is tied to what?

  Satellite

- What is the largest pay-TV system in operation?

  HBO

- Is there a cause-effect relationship between watching violence and committing violent acts? Is there an exception?

  There is no agreement on whether this is true

- Have TV networks attempted to tone down violence in entertainment programs? News?

  Yes   *No*

- What about suits against the networks like the one brought by the parents of the Florida youth who murdered his 83-year-old neighbor? (What was their contention?) (involuntary subliminal TV intoxication)

  It was thrown out

- How can we solve the problem of reporting terrorist acts?

  we can't without censorship

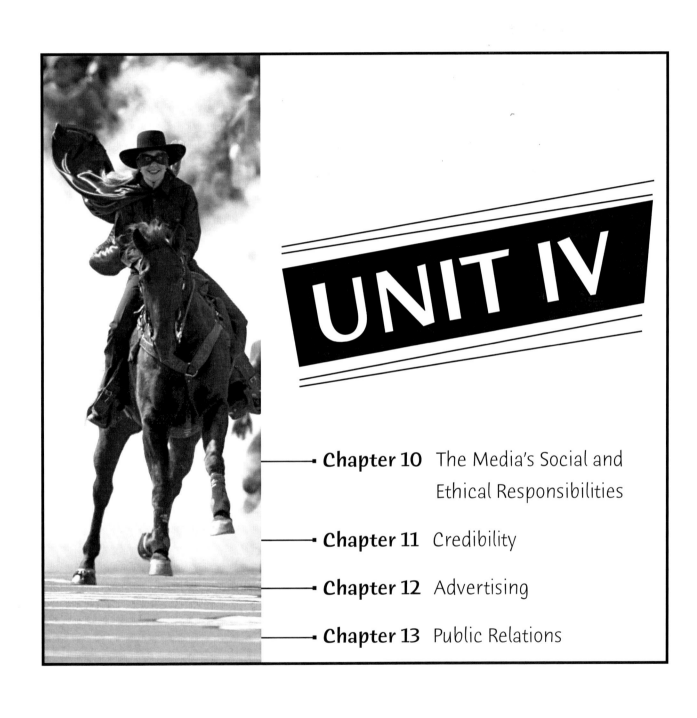

UNIT IV

Chapter 10 The Media's Social and
Ethical Responsibilities

Chapter 11 Credibility

Chapter 12 Advertising

Chapter 13 Public Relations

10 The Media's Social and Ethical Responsibilities

Commission on Freedom of the Press

1. A valuable guide in measuring the balance and depth of a newspaper and its coverage is found in a 1947 report of a group called The Commission on Freedom of the Press. The group was formed to study the alarming number of newspapers that were going out of business, being consolidated, or merged. The fear was that this might harm the free press in this country.

2. The committee did not find that these developments were all that harmful. The main thrust of the report was in identifying characteristics that would make any newspaper a good one. The report remains pertinent today and could actually be applied to all media—not just newspapers.
   a. A truthful, comprehensive, and intelligent account of the day's events in a context, which gives them meaning.
   b. A forum for the exchange of comment and criticism.
   c. The projection of a representative picture of the constituent groups in society.
   d. The presentation and clarification of the goals and values of society.
   e. Full access to the day's intelligence. In this study we will look at the way the media is responding to such social issues as the portrayal of violence, sex, and obscenity, and the standards of good taste and conduct.

Media Ethics

1. The performance of the media in the past three decades has left a lot to be desired. As a result the mass media do not have high rankings with the general public in the areas of professionalism and believability.

2. The 24/7 cable networks have contributed to this problem because their on-air personalities have blurred the lines between reporting the news and inserting personal opinions and bias.

3. Mainstream media have often crossed the line between news and entertainment, influenced by so-called news programs that contain a mixture of news, gossip, rumors, and sensationalism.

Major Problem Areas

1. The cultivation of sources—"A reporter is only as good as his or her contacts."
2. Confidentiality—protecting sources.
3. Conflicts of interest.
4. Gifts and subsidies—"Nothing of value should be accepted."

Discussion

In 1986, The Disney Corporation invited approximately 5,000 media representatives on an all-expenses-paid trip to Disney World for a 15th anniversary party outside Orlando. Estimates were that this cost Disney approximately $8 million. From a public relations standpoint, this was probably a smart idea in that Disney got 10 times the publicity that they would have received if they had simply purchased $8 million worth of advertising. But what about the journalistic community? Is this ethical?

EXAMPLES ## Examples of Concern

❶ The public takes a dim view of the "wolf pack mentality" of the media in certain high profile stories. It appears that the media simply descend on individuals, shove microphones in their faces and demand answers to their questions.

❷ There is the famous story of Washington Post reporter Janet Cooke who wrote a story about an 8-year-old heroin addict and later admitted that her story was a hoax, prompting her dismissal and the return of a Pulitzer Prize in 1981.

❸ Mike Barnicle resigned from the Boston Globe while on a two-month suspension after he was accused of stealing material and lying about his sources.

❹ Jayson Blair, a reporter for the New York Times, resigned May 1, 2003 after it was found that he had taken material from other newspapers and claimed it as his own. In 36 of 73 articles written from October to his resignation, delinquent reporting was found. That's 49% of the time.

❺ Howard Kurtz of the Washington Post resigned in May 2003, after it was discovered that he hired an intern to do his reporting for him. He wrote stories about people he had never actually interviewed and about places he's never seen.

❻ In 1992, NBC Dateline faked a truck explosion for a report about the dangers of crashes involving General Motors pickups. GM sued before NBC finally broadcast a retraction and News President Michael Gartner resigned.

❼ In June 1998, CNN broadcast report that claimed U.S. forces had used the nerve gas Sarin in 1970 while attacking a village in Laos. Time also carried the story. In early June CNN and Time retracted the stories and an independent investigation. Co-producers April Oliver and Jack Smith were fired and Peter Arnett was reprimanded. His contract was not renewed.

8. CBS reporter Dan Rather did a story on *60 Minutes* that President George Bush had not fulfilled his National Guard obligations in the 1960s. Later their source proved to be questionable, as did much of the information. Rather apologized on the air and CBS fired most of the participants. Rather later retired. The question most asked was why CBS was so hell-bent on airing this story without properly checking their information. We will discuss this in our credibility discussion.

9. Photographs: Whether to publish newsworthy pictures that a sure to offend some readers constitutes a dilemma for editors. Photos of the 9-11 tragedy evoked sharp criticism. Ethical issues such as those surrounding the use of video and photographic images of Daniel Pearl will continue to arise.

10. Computer Imaging of Photographs—altering photos

11. Re-creation: The uses of the technique of re-creation, in which actors dramatize news events, have evoked considerable protest. Critics say this blurs the lines between news and entertainment.

12. Reporting about an individual who has contracted the AIDS virus when that individual does not want the information known.

13. "Outing" homosexuals.

Codes of Ethics

1. In 1973, The Society of Professional Journalists broke new ground with the introduction of a new code of ethics. It ends with the statement that "no code of ethics can prejudge every situation; thus common sense and good judgment are required in applying ethical principles."

2. Journalists and journalism educators have mixed feelings about codes of ethics.

3. More than one of every three editors reported that at least one ethics violation had occurred at their papers during the last three years.

4. PRSSA is the only professional communications organization that has created a grievance procedure taking action against members on ethical grounds.

Efforts to Improve

1. Various professional organizations, like the Society of Professional Journalists, are constantly making efforts to clean up their profession.

2. Part of the problem is that these professional organizations are voluntary and have no lawmaking authority.

3. There are also First Amendment considerations. Opponents feel they are a threat to freedom of the press.

4. In the early 1980s, the National Association of Broadcasters developed a Seal of Approval, which was a code of acceptable standards.

5. It was voluntary and finally dropped when the courts found that some sections conflicted with federal antitrust laws.

Advertising

1. The Federal Trade Commission was given authority to regulate advertising in 1938.

2. The American Advertising Federation created the National Advertising Review Board in 1971, which reviews complaints in private, and, failing to get compliance from the advertisers, publicly announces its decisions.

Public Relations

1. The Public Relations Society of America has a certification program that requires an individual to submit work, take exams, and get endorsements.

2. So does the International Association of Business Communicators.

3. Both groups comprise only a small fraction of the total numbers in PR.

11 Credibility

Introduction

1. Credibility means believability.

2. Another key word is perception. Perception is reality to most people and this can cause big credibility problems. Despite what the facts are in any given situation, perception is the key to understanding why public confidence is lacking when it comes to the media.

3. The mass media during the era of Vietnam and Watergate came under the most severe attacks from the public and the federal government since the days of the Revolution and the Civil War. It seems that a "cult of disbelief" has developed since the 1960s.

4. The government and the press have always been adversaries. That is considered healthy. The press always wants to know more than the government wants to tell, so an adversarial relationship has developed over the years.

5. A credibility gap opened between the government and the public in the 1950s and especially in the 1960s during the Vietnam War.

6. Still another credibility gap opened between the media and the public because of so much bad news that people did not want to believe.

7. The public generally supports the concept of a free press and the watchdog role of the press far more than it approves of the performance of the press.

8. Polls have generally found:
    a. Americans are closely divided on the issue of fairness in the media.
    b. Americans are generally quick to criticize the way news is handled.
    c. Americans do not want to tamper with the press and/or its Constitutional safeguards.

9. We will now look at several major events and issues during the last five decades that have caused credibility problems for the press. The key word here is PERCEPTION.

Vietnam (our first televised war)

1. Advisers first arrived in 1955. Our purpose was to stop the spread of Communism. Initially, the press supported the war.

2. Television coverage gave this war a totally different perspective among the American people than did any of the previous wars.

3. By 1963, some members of the U.S. press corps were beginning to challenge the American assumptions regarding Vietnam. They were much criticized for what they wrote, even by their own organizations. David Halberstam, then of the *New York Times,* said America was descending into a quagmire. He was recalled to the states for his efforts.

4. Until the Tet Offensive of 1968, the press heavily supported the war. Then Walter Cronkite, who had early on done several favorable pieces regarding the war, returned and surveyed the situation again. This time he came and in a very important CBS commentary said we ought to end the war and bring our troops home.

5. President Lyndon Johnson escalated the war, but finally choose not to seek re-election as a result of the wide divisions of opinion and general loss in public confidence about the war.

6. President Richard Nixon attempted a withdrawal, following "peace with honor."

7. TV brought it all into our living rooms—for the first time.

The press finds itself in a no win situation.

City Riots

1. Americans were shocked in the mid-1950s when the more peaceful civil rights demonstrations in the South now turned into a protest of the war and many of America's basic institutions erupted across the country—Detroit, Newark, Washington. D.C., the Watts District of Los Angeles, etc.

2. Much criticism was made of TV for giving daily platforms to radical leaders.

3. The national Commission on Civil Disorders criticized the news media for bad judgment, in some instances, of covering the riots in Newark and Detroit in 1967, but found that the media in general tried hard to present a balanced factual account of these riots.

4. The commission generally criticized the media, not for their coverage, but for not properly preparing the American people for an understanding of social unrest.

Student Demonstrations

1. Student militants had observed the attention given the Black movement by the media and sought to now direct nationwide attention to the ills of society as reflected in the universities.

2. Student unrest first erupted at large schools like Berkeley and Columbia.

3. Later they spread to many others like Kent State. At Kent State students, protesting Nixon's handling of the war, burned down an ROTC building on a Friday night in mid-April, 1969. James Rhodes, the governor of Ohio, sent the National Guard to the campus to restore order. The next afternoon a confrontation between the students and the Guard took place and several students were shot and killed.

4. The nation was shocked by this news. But there were two types of reaction. On one hand people said "My God, how could something like this happen in the United States. How could we send armed military forces onto a college campus and murder students. What are we coming to." On the other hand people said "Those students burned down a building and put lives in danger. They were ordered to stop. I'm glad they killed some of them. They should have killed more of these campus bums!" How do you deal with such divergent feelings? Again, the media found themselves in a no-win situation.

The Democratic National Convention of 1968

1. It was an unbelievable performance—the clash of the police and youthful dissenters.

2. Mixed into it were clashes between members of the media and officials of the Democratic National Committee unhappy with media coverage of the convention.

3. The National Commission on the Causes and Prevention of Violence studied the disturbance. Their report described both provocation and retaliation. The report criticized both, but came down heaviest on the police. But the majority of Americans did not agree. Thus, a serious credibility gap between the public and the press developed.

The Government and The Press

1. Another problem for the media is when a confrontation takes place between a government leader and the media. This forces the public to choose sides. Again, media credibility suffers.

2. Throughout history, presidents have clashed with the media: Abraham Lincoln complained about coverage of his Civil War generals. Theodore Roosevelt objected to press accounts related to the purchase of the Panama Canal. Lyndon Johnson criticized the reporting of the Vietnam War.

Richard Nixon

1. Beaten narrowly in 1960, he announced that "You won't have Richard Nixon to kick around anymore" following his loss in the California governor's race of 1962. He felt as though the press was against him.

2. He staged a comeback following the Goldwater debacle of 1964 and got the nomination for president in 1968.

3. The "new" Nixon used TV very effectively by staging interviews with friendly interviewers.

4. When elected, he used the prime time appearance instead of the press conference to communicate. The networks would then offer analysis of what Nixon had said featuring their top news reporters. This angered Nixon.

5. He apparently had a sincere distrust for the press and began a series of moves as early as 1969 to counterattack "his enemies" in the media.

The Agnew Criticisms

1. In 1969, Nixon sent his vice president, Spiro Agnew, after the media. He charged the TV networks with failing to provide "a wall of separation between news and comment." He attacked papers such as the New York Times and Washington Post as having a preponderance of "Eastern Establishment liberal bias."

2. These criticisms came in two speeches and in one speech he referred to the dependence of broadcast stations upon government licensing. He disclaimed any thought of censorship, but some saw in the remarks an implied threat.

3. Research done following the speeches indicated a definite softening of administration criticism and an approach toward "safe handling" of news. In other words, he intimidated the news media.

The Pentagon Papers

1. In June of 1971, the *New York Times* began publishing the famed "Pentagon Papers". Daniel Ellsberg, an employee, who turned them over to reporters from the *Times,* stole the papers from the defense department. *The Washington Post* soon followed. The administration sought and got a temporary restraining order to stop said publication, which was upheld by the Supreme Court, 5-4—a shocking setback for the press.

2. Finally, the Court ruled 6-3 that the government had failed to show how publishing these papers endangered national security and lifted the restraining order. This represented the first time in the history of the nation that the executive branch had successfully invoked prior restraint upon the press, even if it was for a limited period of time.

3. Afterwards, Nixon instituted wiretapping searches to plug security leaks.

4. When the FBI balked at these procedures, Nixon created the infamous White House "plumbers" unit who staged a break-in at the office of Daniel Ellsberg's psychiatrist and, later, at the Watergate Hotel.

"The Selling of the Pentagon"

1. The CBS-TV program contended that the Department of Defense spent millions promoting its activities and political points of view despite a presidential directive to end these practices.

2. CBS President Frank Stanton refused to allow out-takes of the program to be turned over to a Congressional investigation committee. The House declined to cite Stanton and CBS for contempt.

3. Had they cited him for contempt the issue would have, no doubt, wound up at the door of the U.S. Supreme Court.

Watergate

1. The role of Bob Woodward and Carl Bernstein in researching and reporting the Watergate story from June 1972 until March 1973 resulted in constant denial and criticism from the White House.

2. Then James McCord's letter to Judge John Sirica in March, 1973 began to unravel the story.

3. The Ervin Committee hearings in the summer of 1973, followed by the House Judiciary Committee hearings, finally began to focus on the truth.

4. Nixon resigned on August 8, 1974.

5. The press finally came out ahead as public opinion slowly changed. But it was a painful process and a bittersweet victory. Polls taken indicated that close to 20% of the public felt as though Nixon had been hounded out of office by the liberal press.

Ronald Reagan and The Press

1. Reagan was generally very effective in winning public support and approval for his programs.

2. He had a "take charge" aura about him that people liked. He also took a rigid anti-communist stance portraying the **Soviet Union as an "evil empire."**

3. His decision not to include the press in the invasion of **Grenada** resulted in wide-spread criticism by the news media, but approval by the public. Secretary of State George Shultz defended this exclusion of reporters by saying that "in World War II reporters were involved all along. **And on the whole, they were on our side."**

4. The press was informed of the attack on Libya. Still there was extensive press criticism of the attacks as well as Reagan's insistence on military support of the Contras seeking overthrow of the Nicaraguan government. Reagan maintained a very high level of public approval in the opinion polls.

5. He did not fare quite as well in the **Iran-Contra arms deal.**

6. In this instance our government sold arms to Iran, a nation that had kidnapped our diplomats and one we had labeled a "terrorist nation." We then took the money and gave it to the Contras in Nicaragua, an action prohibited by Congress.

7. Reagan accused the press of thwarting the release of two U.S. hostages in Lebanon by releasing the story of the arms deals. The press responded that: "The press didn't sell arms to the Iranians. The press didn't give the money to the Contras, the press just reported it."

6. The hearings conducted by the joint House and Senate judiciary committees in the summer of 1987 produced a little more than Congress bargained for in Col. Oliver North. He was the operative who sold the arms and gave the money to the Contras. He came across as very articulate, intelligent and patriotic.

7. Reagan went out of office with the highest approval rating of any two-term president in our history.

George H.W. Bush

1. President Bush got off to a good start with the press by holding 32 press conferences in his first year as opposed to Reagan's 5.

2. Events in Eastern Europe also gave him a boost—Poland, Hungary, Czechoslovakia, Bulgaria, Romania, East Berlin, and the Berlin Wall.

3. In December, 1989, Bush ordered an invasion of Panama with the intent of capturing General Manuel Noriega.

4. Two hours after the assault began, 16 reporters and photographers were flown aboard Air Force C-141 to Panama. This was pool coverage.

5. But they were sequestered in a military facility during the first 36 hours of fighting and were not able to produce eyewitness accounts of the fighting.

6. Concern for safety was the primary reason given by Secretary of Defense Dick Cheney—but poor leadership by his public affairs people—not military leaders—caused the pool failure.

7. The Pentagon later stated it was committed to the pool and agreed to a number of recommendations for future conflicts.

8. Despite criticism, some in the press, public opinion polls stood heavily in Bush's favor.

9. In the Persian Gulf War the Department of Defense issued the following guidelines:
   a. a pool system strictly controlling the number of journalists covering combat units.
   b. review of stories, photos, and video by military official before the reports were sent.
   c. restrictions on reporting in the States.

10. The press was highly displeased with these restrictions but 83% of the general public approved restrictions on war news coverage.

11. In 1992, news executives and defense officials agreed on guidelines for future conflicts but the Pentagon retained its option to review news material.

The 1992 Presidential Campaign

1. President Bush and independent candidate Ross Perot attacked political reporters frequently during the latter stages of the campaign.

2. The public generally approved of the coverage and thought it was fair. Thirty-five percent thought the press was unfair to Bush.

3. Polls also showed that most reporters and editors supported Bill Clinton.

The 2000 Election

1. The 2000 Election between Vice President Al Gore and Texas Governor George W. Bush was the closest in history. The outcome hung in the balance for over a month while attorneys for both candidates battled over the outcome of the vote in the state of Florida.

2. Initially, the networks called the state for Gore, then backed off. Later, they called it for Bush. Then they backed off again. All the networks had egg on their faces over this performance.

3. It was called the Hanging Chad election because Florida used punch card ballots and there were claims that voters were confused and voted for the wrong person. There were massive recounts.

4. The cable networks covered these recounts and court battles 24/7.

The 2004 Election

1. This election saw the introduction of the so-called 527 organizations, representing the migration of soft money to "independent" partisan organizations called 527s (Section 527 of the IRS code). These organizations are allowed to purchase advertising and are given the right to raise money and campaign for candidates outside the restrictions placed on political parties.

2. One example is Michael Moore's Documentary, *Fahrenheit 911,* which was highly critical of George W. Bush.

3. Another example is the Swift Boat Vets, Vietnam veterans highly critical of Senator John Kerry, Bush's opponent.

4. Then there was the CBS *60 Minutes* broadcast in which Dan Rather accused Bush of not fulfilling his National Guard obligations during the Vietnam War.

5. The CBS documents suggested that Bush had disobeyed a direct order to attend a physical exam, and that there were other lapses in his performance. One memo also indicated that powerful allies of the Bush family were pressuring the guard to "sugar coat" any investigation of his service.

6. Skeptics immediately seized on the typing in the memos, which included a super-scripted "th" not found on all 1970s-era typewriters.

7. The chief source for this story was Bill Burkett, a former Texas National Guard official and a Kerry supporter.

8. CBS initially stood by their story, then announced that it could not prove the authenticity of documents used in the story and that the story was a "mistake" that CBS regretted.

9. CBS Anchor Rather apologized on the air and said "after extensive additional interviews, I no longer have the confidence in these documents that would allow us to continue vouching for them journalistically . I find we have been misled on the key question of how our source for the documents came into possession of these papers. We made a mistake in judgment, and for that I am sorry."

10. The network fired Mary Mapes, the producer directly responsible for the story, and asked three senior news executive to resign. This came following an independent investigation that was sharply critical of the manner in which CBS handled he story.

11. Rather, who had planned to retire, announced he would retire in March, 2005.

12. Jack Kelley, a *USA Today* reporter who fabricated and plagiarized stories for at least 12 years, resigned in 2003. A review of more than 1,400 stories he wrote during his 21 years at *USA Today* revealed a pattern of lies and deceit that began in 1991 when he started reporting regularly from overseas.

The Media and Eliot Spitzer (*Wall Street Journal*)

1. Eliot Spitzer was attorney general of New York in the early 2000s. He regularly made national headlines with his attacks on various corporations.

2. As New York Attorney General he portrayed himself as the moral avenger—the slayer of the fat cat on behalf of the little guy.

3. *Time* called him the Crusader of the Year. *Fortune* called him The Enforcer. *Atlantic* called him a rock star.

4. Journalists are to keep tabs on public officials (the watchdog theory). In this case he was the fair-haired boy and got favorable treatment.

5. He doted out scoops to favored reporters. They repaid him with allegiance. News organizations that criticized him were cut off.

6. Reporters became his accomplices and ran with what he handed them.

EXAMPLES John Whitehead, the former Goldman Sachs chief, published a guest editorial in the *Wall Street Journal* for what Whitehead considered an unscrupulously zealous pursuit of AIG CEO Maurice "Hank" Greenberg.

Spitzer called and threatened him for this, telling him "I will be coming after you." "You will pay the price. This is only the beginning and you will pay dearly for what you have done."

Spitzer then leaked a report to the press that a few weeks after the op-ed piece ran in the WSJ, Greenberg had given $25 million to the World Center Memorial Foundation, a group Whitehead chaired. It was unfounded. It was a smear and the press ran with it.

7. He routinely used the extraordinary threat of indicting entire firms, a financial death sentence, to force the dismissal of executives, such as Greenberg. He routinely leaked to the press e-mails obtained with subpoena power to build public animosity against companies and executives.

8. In the case of Greenberg, he went on national television to accuse the AIG founder of "illegal" behavior. However, he never indicted Greenberg because he could not prove his charges. He never apologized, either.

9. Spitzer's main offense as a prosecutor is that he violated the basic rules of fairness and due process: Innocent until proven guilty; the right to your day in court.

10. The Spitzer method was to target public companies and officials, leak allegations and out-of-context e-mails to a compliant press, watch the stock price fall, threaten a corporate indictment and then move in for a quick settlement kill. There was rarely a trial, fair or unfair, involved.

11. Most of his high-profile charges have gone up in smoke. Time and time again judges have thrown out his cases.

12. In other words, instead of serving as a watchdog of public officials, the press served as his booster and promoter despite obvious warning signals that not all was well.

Political Endorsement

A look at national political campaigns since 1932 shows that however one-sided newspapers lined up editorially, they did not do so in their news columns. The weight of the evidence in various studies made of press performance in covering recent campaigns shows a reasonably creditable job on the news pages. The endorsements were as follows:

Year	Republican	Democrat
1932	Hoover 55	Roosevelt 38—Roosevelt
1940	Willkie 50	Roosevelt 25.2—Roosevelt
1944	Dewey 55	Roosevelt 17.7—Roosevelt
1948	Dewey 78.5	Truman 10—Truman
1952	Eisenhower 72	Stevenson 10.8—Eisenhower
1956	Eisenhower 72	Stevenson 13—Eisenhower
1960	Nixon 70.9	Kennedy 15.8—Kennedy
1964	Goldwater 21.5	Johnson 61.5—Johnson
1968	Nixon 56	Humphrey 15—Nixon
1972	Nixon 93	McGovern 5—Nixon
1976	Ford 62.2	Carter 22.8—Carter
1980	Reagan 48.6	Carter 21.5—Reagan
1984	Reagan 51.6	Mondale 21.3—Reagan
1988	Bush 80	Dukakis 20—Bush
1992	Bush 60	Clinton 40—Clinton
1996	Dole 60	Clinton 40—Clinton
2000	Bush 65	Gore 35

Democrats have won 9 of these 18 elections

1. It would be noted in passing that American readers do not support newspapers purely on political grounds.

2. Not to be discounted are the numerous studies that show that newspaper editorials do not deserve the credit they have been given for influencing public opinion on political questions. Groups, associations, and social pressures more strongly affect voting behavior. The direct broadcast of speeches also influences the voter. Magazines, especially the quarterlies and quality monthlies, are primary sources of information for many people.

3. The key issue here is the treatment that candidates receive on the news pages—not the editorial pages. Newspapers have generally provided very balanced coverage here with some notable exceptions.

4. The criticism aimed at newspapers because of these endorsements have caused many newspapers to shy away from doing this.

12 Advertising

What is Advertising?

It Is Different Things to Different People

1. To you and me it is something that tells us about a new product or service; offers us a second pizza for a penny; tells us where we can buy meat at the best price.

2. To a manufacturer it is a means of telling distributors and consumers about their new product—to presell the goods.

3. To a retailer it is a way of telling people in a community to come and purchase a product in a specific store; to bring in traffic; to make sales; and to make profit.

4. A politician uses advertising to get elected.

5. A charitable organization seeks funds to carry out its work.

6. A governmental organization uses it to recruit personnel.

7. Radio and TV stations depend on it for all of their revenue.

8. Newspapers and magazines get most of their income from it.

9. Many people work in advertising to earn their living and seek success as do people in farming, banking, manufacturing, etc.

10. To some, it is often dishonest, misleading, and threatening to the general public.

11. You may see it as a field of study.

Advertising Today

1. Distribution has replaced production as the principal task of maintaining a high level of employment and general prosperity—this depends largely upon effective use of advertising in the media.

2. In 1947 American business spent slightly over $4 billion to promote its wares. By 1965 advertising exceeded $13 billion a year. In 1978, $37 billion. In 1982, $57 billion. Today, $443 billion with 400,000 employees.

3. Every person in this country is exposed to no fewer than 500 advertisements each day.

The History of Advertising

1. Advertising is as old as civilization itself.

2. The development of advertising in our country paralleled the growth of mass production, mass transportation, and mass selling. At first, advertising was local, appearing on handbills, posters, and then in newspapers. Ben Franklin is credited with using some of the early effective advertising in his newspaper.

3. The advent of railroad transportation, about 1840, enabled manufacturers to distribute their products widely. National advertising resulted. Ad agencies began to appear in the 1840s. Volney B. Palmer is generally credited with starting the first agency in 1840. Early agencies served primarily as publishers' representatives by contracting for space in various publications, which were then sold at a higher price to advertisers. By 1880 they began to buy space in the interest of clients.

4. By the turn of the century, advertising and journalism were on their way toward becoming today's mass media of communications. There were also problems.

5. This was the period of the "huckster" proving that "there is a sucker born every minute." Efforts were made to regulate deceptive and exaggerating advertising.

6. The Pure Food and Drug Act was, to some degree, aimed at the patent medicine business, which was one of the strong early advertisers.

7. To standardize and raise ethical practices, the first Better Business Bureau was formed in 1913 to promote truthful advertising.

8. In 1914, the Audit Bureau of Circulation was formed to assure accurate periodical audits and statements of newspaper and magazine circulations.

9. Radio in the 1920s gave an added dimension to advertising, as we have already discussed.

10. Advertising fought to hold its own during the depression of the 1930s.

11. The Wheeler-Lea Act of 1938 was passed to protect the consumer against false advertising. It gave regulatory authority over advertising to the FTC.

12. Advertising's success in selling war bonds and other patriotic causes during World War II demonstrated its ability to sell ideas as well as products and services.

13. The War Advertising Council spearheaded this movement and has been continued as the Advertising Council, Inc. (Smokey the Bear, United Negro College Fund, Red Cross, etc.). Each year the media donate more than $800 million in time and space to support these campaigns.

14. Postwar developments in advertising have included: (Agee, Ault and Emery)
    a. Growth in the size and number of agencies.
    b. Availability of television as a new selling device.

    c. Use of research to provide facts about products and to discover motivations of consumers.

    d. Greater creativity in advertising.

    e. Expansion of American agencies overseas to tie in with the growing world economy.

    f. Increased effort for self-improvement, self-criticism, and ultimately, professionalization.

15. The 1950s was the "product era" as compared with the "image era" of the 1960s. Comparative advertising or positioning highlighted the 1970s along with the use of the computer to provide analysis for marketing. (Agee, Ault and Emery)

16. Creativity became the all-important characteristic of successful ad people. (Agee, Ault and Emery).

17. In a media-oriented society, many companies found it necessary to "position" a product in the public's mind—a position taking into consideration not only the product's own strengths and weakness, but those of its competitors as well. This is called "comparative advertising" and it was encouraged by the FTC. (Agee, Ault and Emery).

18. We also saw the use of advocacy advertising in the 1980s, in which corporations run paid ads that take sides on important issues. Some respond to what they consider unfair treatment by the media. (Agee, Ault and Emery).

19. We have already talked about the increased emphasis on the use of demographics and target marketing, which also became highly emphasized in the 1980s. The 1980s was also a time when agencies accelerated the trend to become worldwide organizations through a series of mergers and joint agreements.

20. Because of business slowdowns during the early 1980s, many commercials of a humorous, awareness, and image-building variety were giving way to "hard sell" advertisements.

Current Trends in Advertising (Agee, Ault and Emery)

1. Concern about the growth of cable and independent stations, coupled with the heavy use of videocassette records—the splintered audience.

2. Clutter—hundreds of new products.

3. Zapping.

4. Loss of ad revenue to sales promotion firms that devise cents-off coupons.

5. More sophisticated targeting of market segments.

6. Growth in minority populations—during the 1990s, more than 85% of all growth.

7. Combining other expertise into the advertising agency to combat in-house agencies. *Example:* acquisition of direct mail operations.

8. Global advertising—expansion of business worldwide.

9. Talent hunting and "leaner" agencies.

10. Threats to commercial free speech—sales taxes on advertising imposed by states; proposals to make illegal the advertising of alcohol and tobacco.

11. Individuals and organized pressure groups attempting to clean up network TV programs.

12. Online advertising has grown to a $4.33 billion business, still only 2% of the total of all advertising expenditures.

Why Advertising Has Grown

- A psychological maturing—people are willing to seek out information and act.
- Prosperity and the rise of a middle class.
- Improved transportation.
- More credit.
- Less personal selling.
- Better media.
- Better advertising.

The Consumer Movement

1. The powerful consumer movement in this country has drawn a sharp bead on advertising and sought federal sanctions against what it considers to be social ills encouraged by many industry practices.

2. The basic themes of criticism of advertising include: (Agee, Ault and Emery)
   a. It persuades us to buy goods and services we cannot afford.
   b. It appeals primarily to our emotions rather than to our intellect.
   c. It is obtrusive and needlessly repetitious.
   d. Too much is false, deceptive, and in bad taste.
   e. It is expensive and wasteful. Wouldn't it be better to eliminate advertising and cut prices?

Concerns over Ethics and Responsibility in Advertising

1. Concern over misleading advertising.

2. Advertising harmful products, i.e. the $206 billion settlement between cigarette manufactures and 46 states.

3. Not telling people that what they are receiving is advertising.

Reasons For the Criticism (Agee, Ault and Emery)

1. Advertising is a horizontal industry cutting across almost every business—an attack on business results in an attack on advertising.

2. Advertising represents a lot of money—mostly untaxed.

3. Advertising lives in a glass house—it cannot hide its sins.

4. The gray flannel suit image—lavish living, improper tax-deductible expenses.

5. Advertising is not constitutionally protected like journalism by the First Amendment.

Government Regulation

1. The FTC is the principal government agency that regulates advertising. There are many government agencies (IRS, SEC, etc.) that have taken steps to regulate advertising.

2. The FTC was given new powers to regulate business conduct with the FTC Improvement Act of 1975. It has moved against what it calls unfairness in advertising.

3. One of the earliest efforts to regulate advertising was the Pure Food and Drug Act, which curbed patent medicines, particularly fraudulent claims by manufacturers. it was passed in 1906.

4. In 1912, the Federal Post Office Act stipulated that selling devices such as notices and announcements must be clearly labeled as advertisements.

5. The 1914 Audit Bureau of Circulation was organized to standardize and verify publishers' circulation statements for advertisers.

6. The Fair Packaging and Labeling Act of 1966 covered food, drug, and cosmetic packages and the amount of label revision was enormous.

7. In 1968, the Truth in Lending Act was passed, which required disclosure of the annual interest rate on revolving charge accounts.

8. In 1969, a law was passed by Congress that outlawed all cigarette commercials from the air effective in 1971.

9. We have also discussed the counter-advertising proposal of the FTC.

10. In 1973, the Supreme Court ruled that ads are entitled to a degree of First Amendment freedom-of-speech protection.

11. In 1986, the Court banned broadcast commercials for smokeless tobacco products and required warning labels on print tobacco ads.

Advertising Defined (American Marketing Association)

By definition, advertising is (a) paid for, (b) nonpersonal, (c) a presentation of goods, ideas and services, and (d) by an identified sponsor.

1. The advertisers pay for it—it is not free publicity of space in a window.

2. It is nonpersonal—not like face-to-face selling. It has the ability to reach a staggering audience—Roots, the Super Bowl, The World Series, etc.

3. It pertains to more than just tangible goods, but extends to ideas (politics) and services.

4. It is identified—not like a publicity release or propaganda.

Types of Advertising

1. *National advertising* typically uses network television, radio, and magazines. Chief use of this form is to establish the value of a product in the mind of the consumer, and to make its trademark known, so that the consumer will go out and buy the product.

2. *Retail-local advertising* is advertising by a merchant or dealer, which is designed to cause the consumer to buy at his store.

3. *Direct response advertising* is buying directly from the manufacturer

4. *Trade advertising* and business is directed at store owners who are important buyers of goods in quantity, and manufacturers who are buyers of raw materials and other parts that go into the making of their own products. Also, a buyer of machinery and equipment essential to carrying on business.

5. *Professional advertising* is directed by the maker or seller of products to someone who can either recommend their use to others, or who specifies or buys them for use by those whom he advises. This form includes advertising to doctors, dentists, architects, and the like.

6. *Institutional advertising* is designed to sell an entire company or even an idea rather than a specific product.

Advertising's Effects on Consumers

1. It makes people aware of a product or service.
2. It provides price information about a product or service.
3. It provides information about the quality of a product or service.
4. It tries to persuade consumers to identify a product or service with a particular person or activity.

Advertising's Purpose

- Business ads.
- Political ads.
- Public service ads.

Mass versus Targeted Ads

- Ads that target the largest audience possible constitute mass advertising.
- Ads that seek to reach a selected audience are classified as targeted advertising.

Advertising Agencies (contracting with the media for time and space)

1. Usually divided into four departments: creative services, research services marketing or merchandising services, account services, and media buyers.

2. Campaign Research: Study the client's product or service to see the similarities and dissimilarities in relation to its competition.

3. Analyze the present and potential market for which the product or service is intended.
   a. Who uses the product and why?
   b. What are the buying habits of the potential customers?
   c. Who makes the buying decisions?
   d. Which media are these decision makers most likely to rely upon?

e. Which sales appeals are strongest and most persuasive?

f. What attitude problems, if any, must be dealt with

g. What is our competitive situation? What can we do to improve it?

4. Consumer Research

a. Demographics profiles—age, sex, income level, educational level, occupation, size of the family, stage in the family life cycle, religion, and race influence reception of advertising messages and buying decisions.

b. Geographic profiles—sectional differences.

c. Psychographics—lifestyle and sociopsychological factors that influence them.

5. A definite plan is then formulated to be presented to the client.

6. Writes, designs, and illustrates the proposed ads and prepares the broadcast commercials.

7. Produces the ad in final form and contracts for space or time with the media.

8. The key person in servicing an account is the account executive. The AE is the liaison between the agency and the client.

9. Traditionally agencies have charged 15%. (If the ad costs $40,000 the agency collected that amount from the client and paid the medium $34,000 thus earning a $6,000 commission). Also bills for actual costs of preparing the ad plus a service charge of 2.65%.

Departments of the Media

Performs Agency-type Services for a Client

1. Time and space salespeople, employed by all media, attempt to convince agency representatives of the virtues of their medium and call on potential advertisers. They are usually given a client list and are usually paid a base salary plus commission.

2. Researchers collect up-to-date statistics on the markets served by the sales people's newspaper, magazine, or station.

3. Provide many of the services also provided by agencies for smaller advertisers.

4. Newspaper reps sell off a rate card that contains the open rate (top rate for infrequent advertisers), and earned rate (quantity discount).

5. Radio gets 60% of its income from local ads. Radio can be visual. It targets advertising better than TV. **Frequency** is the key.

6. Television presents some different challenges. Most commercials run 15, 20 or 30 seconds, few are longer.

7. In TV a storyboard is developed that contains sketches for each scene and includes copy, music, and special effects. After approval the production work must be done.

8. Major ad agencies contract for network time while national sales reps solicit agencies to obtain spot ads not on the network.

9. Local ads are sold by time solicitors and prepared usually by copywriters employed by the station.

10. Most magazines deal directly with national advertisers or indirectly through reps.

Retail Stores

1. Many large retail stores have their own in-house agency.
2. Sales promotion and marketing specialists work closely with the advertising department to coordinate plans.
3. In many instances the store has to rely and trust the media sales reps who call on them.

Direct Response Advertising

1. In the past direct mail advertising included the publication of coupons in newspapers and magazines as incentives for consumers to make purchases, sample products, and obtain information.
2. In recent years cable TV has stimulated growth in direct-response advertising through the use of 800 telephone numbers that consumers may use to order products. *Example:* QVC.

Industrial and Trade Advertising

1. Ad departments handle inquiries, prepare catalogs, data sheets, direct mail brochures and broadsides, exhibits, and sales promotion materials.
2. Generally, the department handles local advertising for the company's retail outlets and hires an agency to handle trade and national advertising.
3. The industrial ad department may employ one person or as many as 400 or more—typically about six.

Qualifications and Characteristics

1. Advertising is a tough, highly competitive field that is very limited.
2. The rewards are high in agencies, but so is the risk.
3. Agencies are only one aspect of the field. The most jobs are with the media (newspapers, radio and TV, magazines). There are also jobs with retailers, manufacturers, government agencies, nonprofit companies, and private organizations.
4. Types of jobs are extensive. People skilled in writing, selling, research, design, merchandising, law, accounting, photography, music, camera operation, etc., are employed.
5. Ad people receive 10 to 15% higher salaries in metropolitan areas—where the cost of living also is higher.
6. You do not have to know how to draw unless you are in ad art.
7. You do not have to write copy in all ad jobs, but writing is generally considered a basic requirement.
8. It is a good field for women (50%) and minorities.
9. There is constant demand for the creative person.

13 Public Relations

Definition

1. "Public Relations is the management function which evaluates public attitudes, identifies the policies and procedures of an organization with the public interest, and executes a program of action and two-way communication to earn public understanding and acceptance."—Public Relations News

2. "Public relations is a fundamental attitude of mind, a philosophy of management, which deliberately and with enlightened selfishness places the broad interests of the public first in every decision affecting the operation of a business."—Paul Garrett

3. "Public relations is the philosophy of doing things people like and doing them the way people like—and the doing is more important than the saying."

4. "Public relations is that responsibility and function of management which (1) analyzes public interest and determines public attitudes, (2) identifies and interprets policies and programs of an organization and (3) executes a program of action to merit acceptance and good will."—Cyril Plattes of General Mills

5. The public relations function can also be defined as the planned effort to influence and maintain favorable opinion through acceptable performance, honestly presented, and with reliance on two-way communications.

6. No term is more misunderstood than public relations.

7. People often confuse the terms publicity, propaganda, promotion, and public relations.
   a. *Publicity:* news or stories in the mass media about people or organizations.
   b. *Propaganda:* opinion deliberately designed to influence; negative connotations.
   c. *Promotion:* includes all forms of communication other than paid ads that call attention to sales or marketing ideas.
   d. *Public relations:*
      - programming /issues management
      - relationships

- writing and editing
- information
- production
- special events
- speaking
- employee/member relations
- research and evaluation

7. Public relations is not:
   a. Someone who wines and dines media people or customers.
   b. A sales position.
   c. A corporate cover-up.
   d. A back slapper.

8. What is the difference between PR and advertising? Martin Mayer, author of Madison Avenue, USA, makes the distinction clearer: Advertising, whatever its faults, is a relatively open business; its messages appear in paid space or in bought time, and everybody can recognize it as a special pleading. Public relations works behind the scenes; occasionally the hand of the PR man can be seen shifting some bulky fact out of sight, but usually the public relations practitioner stands at the other end of a long rope which winds around several pulleys before it reaches the object of his invisible tugging . . . The advertising man must know how many people he/she can reach with the media, the PR practitioner must know how many people he/she can reach within the media."

History of PR

1. The early antecedents of today's public relations practitioners were:
   a. The pharaohs of ancient Egypt—publicized accomplishments through hieroglyphs on monuments, columns, and temples.
   b. Ancient Greeks and Romans staged events, oratory, etc. for publicity purposes.
   c. Pope Gregory XV in the 17th century established the College of Propaganda to better enable priests to propagate the faith.
   d. Samuel Adams and Thomas Paine used propaganda to fan the flames of war.
   e. Many American Presidents have used public relations
      - Lincoln's Gettysburg Address
      - Franklin Roosevelt's fireside chats on radio
      - John F. Kennedy's inaugural Speech—"Ask Not"
      - Ronald Reagan

2. P. T. Barnum said "there is a sucker born every minute," and generally proved it. He staged events for the purpose of being reported. He used "opinion leaders" (used a slave he claimed was 161 years old and was Washington's maid).

3. Henry Ford "positioned" himself as a leader by doing things first. He used press releases, films, demonstrations, and press conferences and got famous personalities to serve as spokespeople for his products.

4. Teddy Roosevelt was the first president to make extensive use of press conferences and interviews—understanding the value of a presidential tour for publicity purposes.

5. Muckraking, which we have already discussed, probably was the beginning of organized public relations. Ivy Lee, a newspaperman who had covered business news, set up a Business News Bureau to release info to the press on behalf of business corporations. His idea was attractive because business was under attack following the muckraking period. He was really the first PR professional and made the following contributions: (Agee, Ault and Emery)
   a. Business must align itself with the public interest.
   b. PR programs must have the active support of top management.
   c. Communications with the media must be open.
   d. Business must be humanized.

6. We have already discussed the success that the Committee on War Information under George Creel had in World War I in conducting a massive and successful publicity effort to mobilize the public behind the war effort. The results led to the establishment of PR agencies designed to conduct similar campaigns for private citizens.

7. Edward Bernays was one of the leaders in attempting to establish PR as a profession and his activities in the 1920s had significant impact on PR.
   a. Ivory Soap—Procter & Gamble sponsored a national soap-carving contest.
   b. 50th anniversary of Edison's invention—October 21, 1929—got many of the world's utilities to shut off their power all at one time, for one minute.
   c. Helped break the taboo on women smoking by having New York debutantes light "torches of freedom." They were induced to "light up" while marching in New York City's Easter parade as a sign of equality with men.

8. In the 1930s came the development of modern public opinion and marketing surveys.
   a. Theodore Vail of AT&T and Henry Ford were early advocates of systematic feedback from customers.
   b. Real advances were not made in formal public opinion survey research until the 1930s when George Gallup, Elmo Roper, and Claude Robinson began using modern sampling methods and social science statistics.
   c. This provided a tool by which PR counselors and executives could evaluate public attitudes instead of using their own estimates of public opinion. While there is also a degree of possible error present, these surveys have become standard.

9. The growth of public relations in the 1960s and 1970s has been brought about by political and social pressures—consumerism.

10. Today, public relations has become a fully recognized profession:
    a. 250,000 practitioners
    b. 1,500 counseling firms
    c. 4 of 5 companies and trade associations conduct formal PR programs.
    d. Over 15,000 students are currently studying PR in college.

The Function of PR

1. Public relations can be divided into internal and external functions.

2. Internal is where PR must start—the best external PR program in the world is useless unless your employees are being treated right—and are active members of your PR team.

3. An outsider's opinion of the organization will be based almost entirely on the employee he/she knows or encounters.

4. External has two primary divisions:
   a. Community Relations—based on good internal employee relations.
      - Companies and other organizations want to be viewed as good citizens in their communities.
      - The company is dependent upon the community—it provides employees, utilities, police and fire protection, tax breaks, cooperative zoning plans, etc.
      - The company provides the community with jobs, taxes, other economic support, funds and personnel for community projects.
   b. Public information—composed mostly of media relations and publicity.
      - Public relations people must become well acquainted with the media—people they will be dealing with—and with the special editorial characteristics and requirements of each medium.
      - Most of the publicity is generated through press releases or news conferences.

What Do PR People Do? (Confusion)

1. Sometimes PR is divided into the following:
   a. **Counseling (Generalists)**—Giving advice on what to do and what not to do. It is perhaps the most important PR function and sometimes the most difficult function to get management to accept.
      - This is normally a management position.
      - It requires background and experience.
      - The experienced PR professional divides his/her time as follows: techniques 10%, administration 40%, analysis and judgment 50%.
   b. **Staff services (specialists)**—those special skills and techniques that include speeches, press releases, editing publications, special events.
      - This includes the entry-level jobs.
      - This person spends his/her time as follows: judgment 5%, techniques 50%, running like the dickens 45%.

2. An individual in PR must constantly be concerned with the many "publics" that he/she must deal with. These include: employees, stockholders, suppliers, distributors, the community, the government, customers, media. In a given instance a decision made by the company will not please all these publics—such as a price increase. This calls for a value judgment.

3. Generally speaking the public relations process works as follows:
   a. Fact finding and evaluation—requires research.
   b. Formulate policy and recommend what to do
   c. Plan.
   d. Execute.
   e. Assess and evaluate the results.

4. Another way to look at it was described by Bernays as PR Components:
   a. Define your audience.
   b. Research your publics.
   c. Modify your objectives to reach goals that research shows are attainable.
   d. Decide on your strategy.
   e. Set up your themes, symbols, and appeals.
   f. Blueprint an effective organization to carry out the activity.
   g. Chart your plan for both timing and tactics.
   h. Carry out your tactics.

Types of PR Work

Business Corporations (Agee, Ault and Emery)

1. The largest single area of public relations work is in corporate public relations. With few exceptions, U.S. businesses, industries, banks, trade associations, and retail stores employ their own PR department practitioners or hire an outside counseling firm.

2. Businesses which 20 years ago had no one in PR now do. The consumer movement has brought much of this about.

3. Businesses that might have had one PR type 20 years ago now have 25 or more in a well-defined department.

4. About 85% of the 1,500 largest corporations that have planned PR programs have PR departments, often aligned with advertising and personnel departments.

5. The Public Relations Society of America surveyed 166 corporations and found that those with more than a billion dollars in annual sales employed PR staffs averaging 65 persons.

Public Relations Counseling Firms

1. PR agencies range in size from two employees to 2,000, often with advertising services. There are about 1,500 in the U.S. today.

2. About 30% of U.S. companies with PR programs also use the services of public relations counseling agencies.

3. One agency alone employs more than 300 persons.

4. Agencies can offer special assistance in many areas, i.e., crisis management, events management, fund raising, political public relations.

Other Forms of Public Relations

- Associations—trade associations, medical associations, farm co-operatives, labor unions.

- Government—called public information because of federal law—local, regional, state, national. Today some of those involved in government PR are referred to as spin doctors. Also public relations directed at government, i.e., lobbying, government relations.

- Nonprofit—social agencies, health organizations, hospitals, religious, welfare agencies, cultural organizations.

- Education—both secondary and higher education.

- Sports—collegiate and professional.

- Entertainment—publicity.

- Travel.

NOTE: Many of the above include fund raising and events management.

Trends

- Technological changes, i.e., the Internet, e-mail, the World Wide Web.

- Globalization—expansion of public relations activity worldwide.

- Growing business crisis, i.e., Enron, Arthur Andersen, Worldcomm, Martha Stewart and her questionable sale of ImClone stock.

Characteristics for PR Work

1. Basically PR is communications.

2. Because it is important that PR people work with media, it follows that many PR workers are ex-media people—especially newspaper people.

3. The primary skill that a PR professional must have is writing ability—at some point almost all PR communication is reduced to writing.

4. Oral communication ability is also important—increasing as responsibility and authority increase.

5. Have taken a wide range of courses.

6. Good at conceptualizing.

7. Demonstrate teachability.

Professionalism

1. Public relations is not a profession such as medicine and law.

2. Those fields require legal state certification following years of preparation and passing of exams.

3. The PRSA certifies the professionalism of practitioners through a program of accreditation—five years of experience, two sponsors, pass written and oral exams.

4. This represents progress, but not everyone belongs to PRSA.

Criticisms and Challenges

1. Trying to manage or control the news.
2. Attempting to finagle space in news columns to praise clients.
3. Employing pressure, often at the highest level, to affect editorial policy.
4. Being uninformed or indifferent to the media's editorial requirements.
5. Hiring away talented reporters from the media for better paying jobs.

Public Relations and The Mass Media

1. The news media, to a large extent, depend upon the public relations professional to do their job.
2. No medium could afford to support a staff large enough to have experts in every field of human endeavor.
3. Media rely on public relations persons representing companies and institutions to provide the expertise, the background, and the explanations and translations from the language of the experts.
4. Admittedly it is possible for PR people occasionally to take advantage of the media, but professionals who want a long-lasting relationship with the media based on trust can not afford to offend the media in this manner.

UNIT IV: STUDY GUIDE

1. What were the requirements for a press in a free society developed by the Commission on Freedom of the Press in 1947?

2. Describe the ethics problems of (a) Gary Hart (b) Janet Cook.

3. What is the problem with recreation?

4. Describe the PRSA's certification and regulation program.

5. What is the problem in journalism of developing codes or standards of conduct?

Credibility

1. Discuss the impact of perception on media credibility?

2. Discuss the "credibility crisis" of the press in regard to each of the following:

    a. Vietnam

    b. City riots in the 1960s

    c. The Democratic National Convention of 1968

3. Discuss the impact of the following events during Nixon Administration:

   a. The Agnew criticisms of the press

   b. The Pentagon Papers case

   c. "The Selling of the Pentagon" documentary.

4. What initially happens to media credibility when it has a conflict with the government?

5. Describe the impact of the Watergate affair and the role of the media in report it.

6. Why did President Reagan say he did not allow the press to accompany troops in the invasion of Grenada? What was the position of the press?

7. Discuss other credibility problems of the media in regard to presidential endorsements.

Advertising and Public Relations

1. Briefly trace the historical development of advertising.

2. Describe the size and scope of advertising today.

3. Describe what is done in the following areas of advertising: national, retail or local, specialty, mail-order, trade, industrial, professional.

4. What characteristics are important to be successful in advertising?

5. Describe the nature of work performed in the each of the following area:

    a. Ad agencies

    b. Media ad departments

    c. Retail store advertising

    d. Industrial and trade advertising

6. Define advertising (four parts).

7. What is the difference between advertising and public relations?

8. Explain what contributions the following made to public relations:

    a. P. T. Barnum

    b. Ivy Lee

    c. Theodore Roosevelt

    d. Edward Bernays

9. What is the difference between internal and external public relations?

10. What is the difference between counseling and staff services in public relations?

11. What characteristics are important to be successful in public relations?

12. Describe the various types of public relations work done in this country.

UNIT IV: REVIEW QUESTIONS

Ethics

- Do journalists agree that there should be a professional code of ethics?

- Is ethics a problem throughout the field of mass communications or only in certain mediums?

- Who was Janet Cook?

  Reporter from Washington Post who wrote a fraudulant story

- Who was Gary Hart?

  (D) Senator running for president who was found to be having an affair

- List the five requirements for a press in a free society developed by the 1947 Commission on Freedom of the Press. *1. Truthful account of whats going on 2 fair criticism and comment*

- What is recreation and why do journalists have a problem with it?

  recreating a news story   its a dramatization

- Which professional mass comm organization probably does the best job of certifying and regulating its members? *The PRSA*

- What is a junket? *a free trip to journalists*

- Why is self-regulation in the mass comm field difficult? (because of First Amendment protection for freedom of expression. *because of freedom of speech issues*

Credibility

- Why does perception impact media credibility?

  Perception is reality

- What did the Times Mirror study find? (appreciates more than approves)

  The public appreciates more than it approves

- What three things have polls by Gallup and Harris show about the public's opinion of the media?

  we are divided on whether the media is fair   not tampering with the first amendment

- Did the press initially support the Vietnam War?

  yes

- What kind of situation does the press typically find itself in regarding the coverage of emotional issues?

  A No win Situation

- What was the major criticism of the media following research of violence in America cities in the 1960s?

  They failed to prepare Americans

- What happened to news media credibility following the 1968 Democrat Convention?

  It sank to an all time Low

- Is it unusual to have a credibility duel between the press and government? Who does the public initially believe when there is a conflict between the two?

  No not unusual

  the government

- Who did the "hatchet work" for Richard Nixon and what impact did this criticism have on networks?

  V. P. Spiro Agnew

- What happened in the Congressional hearings about the "Selling of the Pentagon" documentary by CBS?

  President of CBS subpoenaed and told to give out files he refused

- Who uncovered the Watergate case? Washington Post/Woodward & Bernstein

- What was the feeling of the public toward the press after Watergate?

  generally credibility was restored

- What was the reason given by President Reagan for not allowing the press to accompany troops in the invasion of Grenada? What did the press think his real reason was?

  He was concerned of their safety
  They thought he was governing media

- Which party's candidate has the press normally endorsed in presidential elections? When and who was the major exception?

  Republicans   *L BJ   1964*

- Based on the results of these elections what can you say about the influence of the newspaper endorsements? (overrated)

- If you are going to make a determination as to whether or not a newspaper is biased toward a political candidate what should be your basis for such a charge?

  What's Not on the editorial page

Advertising History

- How many advertising message are we exposed to daily?

  500

- In the future what age groups will require strategy changes for advertisers?

  45-60 and seniors

- Describe the growth of advertising. What has it paralleled?

  the growth of mass production, transportation, selling

- When did national advertising first develop?

  1840s

- Who is a "Huckster"? What was the Pure Food & Drug Act designed to do?

  Con-artist   *Combat Hucksters*

- What is the Audit Bureau of Circulations?

  Forced publishers to be upfront

- What was the Wheeler-Lee Act?

  gave FTC power over advertising

- Describe the impact of advertising in World War I and World War II.

  It proved advertising and PR works

- After WWII describe the growth of advertising.

  It exploded and spread nationally

- What is the Advertising Council?

  outgrowth of WWII

- What is "positioning"?

  you do something to put yourself of competition

- What have advertising people tried to do in regard to being considered "professional"?

  weed out the Hucksters

Advertising Criticism

- What are the principal criticisms of advertising?

- What is the principal government agency that deals with advertising?

  FTC

- Why have consumer groups targeted advertising? (drawn a sharp bead)

  advertising represents a business

- What is the Truth in Lending Act?

  It forced stores to show balance and Interest on credit cards

Advertising

- What is the definition given in class of advertising (4 parts)?

  paidfor, identified,

- Be able to describe the following forms of advertising: national, retail or local, ~~specialty, mail-order,~~ industrial, trade, professional.

  direct-response

- Describe what the creative department of an ad agency does.

  looks at research art competition to create ad campaign

- How do ad agencies make money?

  take 15% of price

- How competitive is the ad agency business?

  extremely

- What is the role of the account executive in an ad agency?

  liason between client and agency

- What do media sales reps do? (Whom do they call on?) (How do they use a rate card?)

  rep the media on a local level   they provide agency type services for clients

- What is drive time period in radio?

  7 - 9 am   5 - 7 pm

- What is a major difference between advertising rates for newspapers as compared with radio? TV? (radio-TV will offer special rates)

- What are the advantages of radio advertising?

  flexible little production relatively inexpensive

- What is different about industrial advertising?

  doesn't go to consumer

- What is probably the chief characteristic that an ad person needs to have?

  ability to write

- Do you have to draw to be in advertising?

  No

Public Relations: Introduction and History

- What is the difference between advertising and public relations?

  adv you pay for, is non-personal and identified, also sells goods   PR doesn't

- Why is the term public relations misunderstood? (Refer to list of things that PR is not or shouldn't be.)

- Who was P. T. Barnum and what is he credited with saying?

  Huckster - A sucker born every minute

- Who was the first American president to understand the value of the presidency for PR?

  Theodore Roosevelt

- Who was the first public relations practitioner? What three principles did he required that businesses subscribe to before he would work with them? *Ivy Lee*

  align with public interest, they had to listen to him, be open to media, be human

- Who was Edward Bernays? Describe his campaign for Ivory Soap?

  Father of PR   *soap carving contest for kids*

- When did public opinion polling first develop?

- How did consumerism impact on public relations in the last three decades?

  Created jobs for PR

- Is public relations a profession?

  No it's not licensed

- Does the media depend upon public relations?

  yes

Public Relations

- What is internal public relations?

  dealing with employees

- Describe the management level of public relations?

  decision maker

- What is staff services in public relations?

  specialist area / entry level

- What skills should someone who wants to get into public relations develop?

  writing, speaking, creativity

- What does a public relations agency do?

  counsels people on a campaign

- Where does the largest number of individuals work in public relations?

  ~~research, formulate plan,~~ corporate America, corporations

- What are the five steps in the public relations process?

  Research, formulate recommendation, plan

- Why does the government call it public information instead of public relations?

  congress passed laws that make it illegal for propaganda

  PR sounds like Propaganda